HIKIKOMORI

HIKIKOMORI

Adolescence without End

Saitō Tamaki | Translated by Jeffrey Angles

University of Minnesota Press
Minneapolis
London

Published by the University of Minnesota Press
111 Third Avenue South, Suite 290
Minneapolis, MN 55401-2520
http://www.upress.umn.edu

Library of Congress Cataloging-in-Publication Data

    Saitō Tamaki, 1961–
    [Shakaiteki hikikomori. English]
    Hikikomori : adolescence without end / Saitō Tamaki ; translated by Jeffrey Angles.
    First published in Japan in 1998 by PHP Institute, Inc. [as Shakaiteki hikikomori : owaranai shishunki].
    Includes bibliographical references and index.
    ISBN 978-0-8166-5458-1 (hc : alk. paper)
    ISBN 978-0-8166-5459-8 (pb : alk. paper)
    1. Social isolation—Japan.   2. Social isolation.   3. Social distance—Japan.   4. Social distance.   5. Stress in youth—Japan.   6. Stress in youth.   I. Angles, Jeffrey, 1971–   II. Title.
    HM1131.S2413 2013
    302.5'450952—dc23

                                   2012043837

Printed in the United States of America on acid-free paper

The University of Minnesota is an equal-opportunity educator and employer.

25 24 23 22 21   10 9 8 7 6 5

CONTENTS

TRANSLATOR'S INTRODUCTION
How to Diagnose an Invisible Epidemic

Jeffrey Angles

When first published in 1998, this book struck a major nerve in Japan and quickly became a best seller. Although the author, Saitō Tamaki, is currently well known as a major cultural critic and one of the foremost Japanese experts on the psychological problems of youth, at the time he published this book he was still relatively unknown. Saitō had graduated from the medical school at Tsukuba University in 1990 with a grounding in Lacanian psychiatry and was working as a therapist in Sōfūkai Sasaki Hospital in Funabashi, just to the east of Tokyo, when he was struck by a recurring problem among his patients. As he describes in this book, he found himself amazed at the numbers of parents and relatives who came in to consult with him about children who hid themselves away, retreated from school and work, and refused to go outside. These adolescents and young adults had ceased interacting in society and instead stayed nervously cooped up at home with few connections to the outside world. These were not just people suffering from depression, although depression might be linked to their afflictions. Rather, they were suffering a specific, interlocking series of symptoms that could not be easily fit under a single, easily identifiable medical cause. The more Saitō looked into the problem, the more he realized there were untold numbers of young adults throughout society who were living in these sorts of conditions, and over the next several years he dedicated himself to studying, analyzing, and understanding the lives of these people.

As he explains in this book, he and other psychiatrists presented papers and gave lectures about withdrawal and similar, related conditions, but the psychiatric institution in Japan, for the most part, failed to treat withdrawal as a distinct issue and instead treated individual cases on an ad hoc basis. In this book Saitō argues, based on his own clinical experience, that the current diagnostic tools available in the *Diagnostic and Statistical Manual of Mental Disorders, Fourth Edition* or *DSM-IV* (the diagnostic manual published by the American Psychiatric Association and used throughout much of the world) do not account especially well for the cases that he and his colleagues found. The term *social withdrawal,* or *shakaiteki hikikomori,* as it is translated into Japanese, does in fact come from the *DSM-IV*; however, it appears there as a symptom and not as a diagnostic category. Saitō emphasizes that there are many withdrawn young people in Japan who do not seem to be suffering from any other primary mental disturbance. For this reason, he urged the Japanese public and psychiatric world to start thinking about social withdrawal as a distinct phenomenon. In this book he attempts to define the condition, using precise language and case studies. By providing a name and definition for the phenomenon of withdrawal, Saitō worked to bring it to public attention and provoked a firestorm of debate among psychologists, psychiatrists, and counselors.

Indeed, the publication of this book caused a surge of media attention and launched Saitō to a position as the foremost expert in Japan on youth culture and the problem of withdrawal, in particular. His clear, easily understandable description, as well as his urgent insistence that withdrawal is a growing problem that threatens to reach epidemic proportions, made him a media sensation. Popular journals began requesting articles from him, and he became a frequent speaker on television. Since then, he has availed himself of this media attention to spread knowledge about the condition and to make the word *hikikomori* (withdrawal) known throughout the nation. It was largely due to Saitō's success in the media that this word burst into popular circulation and appeared on the lips of journalists, writers, and critics throughout the nation. In short, this book and Saitō's subsequent work and media appearances brought a condition that had been hidden in back rooms and apartments throughout Japan—a silent epidemic of suffering—to the attention of the public.

In this book Saitō does not hazard a guess at the total number of adolescents and young people in Japan who might be living in a state of social withdrawal, but elsewhere, in numerous articles and collections, he has speculated that the number of people living in a state of withdrawal is probably around or even over 1 million.[1] This is an astounding number given that in 2000, the population of the entire Japanese nation was approximately 127 million; in other words, just shy of 1 percent of the entire nation might be living behind closed doors. This number has proved controversial, and some have accused Saitō of engaging in scare tactics, attempting to earn attention for his own work on withdrawal with this dramatic and often-quoted number. In fact, Saitō himself is the first to admit the difficulty in accurately gauging the number of shut-ins, or hikikomori as they quickly came to be called in the Japanese media, and he has stated that his numbers were initially based only on guesses and his own clinical experience.[2] Still, the Japanese Ministry of Health, Labor, and Welfare conducted a survey of public health departments and psychological well-being social centers throughout the country, attempting to identify the number of people living in a state of withdrawal that was not caused by a particular psychological ailment, such as schizophrenia. They located 6,151 people who, in the space of a year, had come or called for consultation with problems that seemed to fit that description. Of them, 57.8 percent were above twenty-one years old, and 23.3 percent were in a deep state of withdrawal that had lasted for more than five years.[3] This is not an overwhelming number, but needless to say, shut-ins do not readily come to doctors to present themselves for treatment, and the parents taking care of children in withdrawal are often too ashamed to talk about them with the outside world. This suggests that the numbers discovered by the Japanese government are only the tiniest tip of the iceberg—a hint at a much larger problem kept mostly out of view.

Saitō has also quoted a study by the organization Rainbow (Niji), run by Ogi Naoki, a frequent speaker on the Japanese educational system and adolescent problems, such as bullying, rebelliousness, and truancy. In 2001 Rainbow published the results of a survey of 2,934 ordinary citizens, primarily people who had come to attend Ogi's lectures. According to this survey, 94.9 percent of respondents knew the word *hikikomori*, 29.2 percent claimed that they knew a young person in withdrawal in their close circle of friends and acquaintances, and 3 percent said that they had a hikikomori child in their own family. Ogi used these results to speculate that the total population of people in withdrawal in Japan ranged somewhere between 800,000 and 1,200,000 people—a number that Saitō saw as support for his own estimates of the overall hikikomori population.[4]

Clearly, these numbers are in no way, shape, or form scientific, considering that they did not come about through a random sample of the Japanese population; however, the very nature of the condition renders the actual number of cases exceedingly difficult to pin down. As Saitō points out in the new preface that he wrote for this English translation, the Japanese government has recently engaged in a number of more scientific surveys. For instance, in 2010, the Japanese Cabinet Office conducted a survey that produced an estimate of nearly 700,000 people in withdrawal in Japan. Still, Saitō argues that because so much shame is associated with withdrawal, the epidemic is likely even more widespread than that. Whether or not one chooses to argue with Saitō's estimate of 1 million people, the unmistakable point he makes in his many publications is that there is a disturbingly large number of people living shut off from society, and because of that, they are almost invisible and exceedingly difficult to account for. More importantly, the problem almost never improves on its own, and since most people in withdrawal are not receiving treatment, the multitudes of people in withdrawal will only continue to grow.

Saitō's work not only helped make the hikikomori issue well known to Japanese readers, situating people in withdrawal as the objects of knowledge for the general population, it also gave people who had withdrawn from society a term that they could use to talk about themselves, thus positioning them as subjects. Saitō has written elsewhere that his patients sometimes commented that before they encountered the word *hikikomori*, they did not have a name for their own actions and suspected that they were alone in their reclusive behavior. This simply led to a greater sense of regret and despair that only aggravated their situations as lonely, hurt individuals.[5] Likewise, families did not have terms to describe the behavior of their reclusive members, but Saitō's 1998 book and the subsequent surge of media attention gave them vocabulary to talk about the subject and let them know that others like them existed throughout the country. As a result, the last decade or so has seen the beginnings of something like a hikikomori identity, as people have started to identify themselves with the condition.

In Japan many people, especially those who are middle-aged or older, are generally hesitant to talk about difficult psychological issues to psychiatrists or counselors—certainly more reticent than North Americans or Europeans, who tend to see counselors, psychologists, and psychiatrists as important health-related resources that one should not necessarily be ashamed of. It is precisely because so many Japanese are hesitant to talk about their personal problems that Saitō emphasizes repeatedly in this book that parents of hikikomori children should seek clinical help themselves, and they should try to join networks for other families with similar problems, thus enabling their own support and healing, which represents an important part of the process. The need to talk about the problem of withdrawal requires language, especially a normalized, clinical vocabulary that can be used to talk about withdrawal without stigma. In this sense, this book and the surge of media attention performed an important social function by giving the Japanese population terminology to talk openly about this issue and how it affects their lives, families, and the nation as a whole.

Interestingly, in this book Saitō tends to avoid using the word *hikikomori* to refer to the person in withdrawal himself or herself. Instead, the word tends to appear largely as a descriptor, as in the phrase *hikikomori seinen* (withdrawn young man). It was around the time of the publication of this book and Saitō's prominence in the media that the word *hikikomori* came to be used as a noun to describe a person in withdrawal. Now, it is not uncommon to hear people in Japan say things like "These days, I've been living a life of a *hikikomori*," thus indicating that the term has gone from being an adjective to a noun describing a person. For instance, Takimoto Tatsuhiko's popular 2002 novel *NHK ni yōkoso (Welcome to the NHK)*, which inspired an even more popular manga series of the same title, is told from the viewpoint of a young man who declares right at the beginning, "I am a *hikikomori*," thus asserting his withdrawn state as something that speaks to the very core of his identity. (Interestingly, Takimoto himself claims to be a hikikomori who has returned to society.) As the issue of withdrawal and its prevalence in Japanese society has become increasingly visible in recent years, it has become possible for people to occupy the space of subject and take on a "hikikomori identity." What was once described just a few years ago as a condition is increasingly read back into the interiority of the individual in that condition.

In many ways this situation is perhaps not unlike the one described in Michel Foucault's *La volonté de savoir (The Will to Knowledge)*, which recounts how certain categories established by psychiatrists to describe what was then seen as aberrant and perverse behavior were then read back into the interiority of the individuals manifesting that behavior, thus establishing a new kind of identity for them. The language of the category came to describe them as people, and in this way the so-called perversion was "implanted" in their very being. In some cases this identity underwent an inversion as the people themselves started to adopt this identity publicly and made it the basis of a social movement. For instance, the group that medical doctors had identified as "homosexuals" adopted this label as an identity that went mainstream and became the basis for political identification and an equal rights movement that sought fairness in the workplace and under the law.

Saitō often emphasizes in this book and others that hikikomori is not exactly an illness or a typology; it is a particular state that develops in conjunction with certain environmental factors and that can be changed through improving communication with the family and the surrounding world. If anything, it is a state that arises in response to perceived setbacks on the path to emotional maturity and independence. The implication would be that one does not necessarily have to read this back into the interiority of the individual as a sign of some unchangeable element of his or her personality. At the same time, the frequency with which this term has come to be used by the general population and even by people in withdrawal themselves suggests that there is a certain slipperiness in the word *hikikomori* that could have important implications as discourse about withdrawal continues to evolve. One sees hints of this in an article published in London in the *Independent* in 2001. The article tells the story of a young man who lived holed up in his room until he happened across a television program about Saitō and his work on withdrawal. The young man stated, "I tried not to admit it at first, but I realized that there were other people out there, experiencing the same thing as me." His parents urged him to go for therapeutic consultation, and he consented to start treatment and eventually joined a day-care center run by Saitō where the young man could interact with other people recovering from a similar situation. Finding similar people with whom he could interact was the most important step in his recovery. He stated that until then, "I had no word for what I was experiencing, so I couldn't explain it to anyone else. But now we have the word—hikikomori. That is the most important thing."[6]

Through media reports like this one about the hikikomori situation in Japan, the word has slowly crept into English. The third edition of the *Oxford English Dictionary* published in 2010 includes an entry for *hikikomori* that explains it as follows: "In Japan: abnormal avoidance of social contact; acute social withdrawal; (also) a person, typically an adolescent male, engaging in this; a recluse, a shut-in." The first example of its usage in the *OED* comes from an article published in the *Japan Christian Review* in 1998, the same year Saitō published this book. A quick examination of LexisNexis shows hundreds of articles published in the English-language media on the subject, but almost every single one is related in some way or another to Japan.

This begs the important question of whether withdrawal or hikikomori is a specifically Japanese problem. As the translator of this book, I have been hesitant to overuse the word *hikikomori* in the body of the main text, fearing that the transliterated Japanese word would give the impression that it is a problem confined only to Japan—a notion that Saitō has repeatedly rejected. In part I, chapter 4, Saitō surveys the opinions of psychiatric colleagues from around the world. The opinions that he receives are too impressionistic and far too few to be conclusive in any way, but he uses them nonetheless as evidence to state that social withdrawal is not only a Japanese problem—just as the origin of the expression in English would suggest. Withdrawal is a process of the human psyche, but given that social withdrawal has to do with problems in adjusting to society, it only makes sense that individual cases reflect issues in the surrounding society. In other words, withdrawal is a universal phenomenon, but the particular form in which withdrawal manifests itself in Japan does have to do with Japanese or perhaps even East Asian culture more broadly. In the final chapter of this book, Saitō argues that the contemporary educational system is a big part of the problem, especially policies that place students in intense competition with one another while maintaining the outward illusion that the students are all supposed to be equal.

Some of the other factors that Saitō has pointed to in his other work have to do with the nature of the East Asian family and the question of what it means to be an adult. (As Saitō notes in the new preface written for this translation, he has become aware in recent years that Korea is another nation that is home to a large number of people in withdrawal.) Saitō has written about the role of the family elsewhere, and perhaps some of those comments are worth quoting at length. The following passage comes from the 2002 book *"Hikikomori" kyūshutsu manyuaru (How to Rescue Your Child from "Hikikomori")*.

> It goes without saying that in the West, "establishing oneself as an individual" is a self-evident premise. I know that in the West, the model of establishing oneself involves leaving the household. I say this because when a child comes of age, he or she is often compelled to separate from his or her parents and go off to live as an individual.
>
> In contrast, the image that Japanese have of establishing oneself is a model that involves "filial piety" *(oya kōkō)*. It is even the case that children will live with their parents and take care of them, and through that, they will become complete as a person for the first time; in other words, they will establish themselves. Of course, the influence of Confucian culture, which was first imported from China, then underwent far-reaching reforms during and following the Meiji Period [1868–1912], is probably quite large.
>
> Another even more unique Japanese element is the culture of *amae* [dependency or reliance] that Doi Takeo wrote about.[7] Doesn't it seem that the kind of filial relationship that Japanese

see as most desirable involves mutual reliance and indulgence? Establishing oneself does not necessarily involve leaving the home, and there is a greater acceptance of people living together under the same roof. For instance, one can see this cultural element at work in the rise of "parasite singles" (unmarried people who continue to live with their parents even after they graduate, relying on their parents for the basic conditions of their existence), which are said to number as many as ten million. If one of the most desirable models of establishing oneself involves filial piety, this probably means that the relationships will develop into ones of "dependence/indulging." . . .

On the other hand, if one were to look at the situation in comparison with other Asian societies, first and foremost, one must not ignore the economic component. In the past, I have sent out questions about my hikikomori cases by e-mail to psychiatrists from all over the world. At that time, one psychiatrist from Thailand sent me back the query "How do they go about putting food on the table?"

This is a rather simple question—or rather, one that is quite straightforward. The reason I say this is because one of the conditions for the rise in numbers of hikikomori is an economic status that would allow the family to continue to support the unemployed child even after he or she becomes an adult.[8]

In other words, Saitō proposes that there is a group of factors at work in producing high numbers of hikikomori cases in Japan: the assumption that it is fine or even desirable for a child to continue to live with his or her parents into adulthood, a cultural propensity to develop relationships of dependency (*amae*) in which the parents take care of the child and the child relies on the parents in an unequal and sometimes codependent form of love, and a level of wealth that allows parents to take continue taking care of their children even when the child has reached physical maturity. This combination of factors works to allow certain children to stay in a position of emotional and economic dependence, even immaturity. The result is a somewhat higher likelihood that children will remain in a continued, artificially prolonged state of adolescence.

There, in essence, is the relevance of this book for students and scholars of Japanese society and culture, and Japanese subcultures, in particular. In this book Saitō is careful to prudently limit the scope of his focus to the definition and treatment of social withdrawal, rather than engage in an overarching general critique of Japanese society, which *does* continue to produce a majority of mature, relatively well-adjusted individuals. Still, as he himself would note, there is a particular combination of socioeconomic factors in Japan that, when coupled with problems in the operations of the individual family and a systemic failure to provide enough resources for the psychological care of its citizens, has led to a rise in this condition. On the one hand, Saitō's main position is that social withdrawal is not a phenomenon found solely in Japan, and he is resistant to the view that somehow Japanese society is itself pathological in nature—a view dramatically reflected, for instance, in *Shutting out the Sun: How Japan Created Its Own Lost Generation,* Michael Zielenziger's attention-grabbing book about hikikomori published in 2006. On the other hand, if one reads between the lines of this book, one finds the implication that the nature of familial interactions commonly seen in Japan has helped incubate the problem and therefore bears some reconsideration.

If the crux of the problem lies in the family and the withdrawn individual's own perceived inability to cope with the world, this still does not mean that parents should turn their children out, force them to get a job, or try to make them "grow up." Saitō writes that such extreme reactions only produce heartache, failure, or worse yet, disaster. In the second half of this book, Saitō lays out a plan that involves modifying the nature of the parent–child relationship to restore meaningful communication—in other words, helping the hikikomori child interact with the parents in a more adult fashion—as a step toward engaging with the world in a more meaningful way. This represents, in Saitō's eyes, a critical step toward emotional adulthood.

Clearly, parents and their modes of interacting with their children are part of the problem, but Saitō never becomes accusatory in this book. No doubt, one reason he did not lay blame explicitly with problematic parent–child relationships has to do with the fact that the principal audience consists of the families of hikikomori themselves. Saitō argues that to resocialize a person who has gone into withdrawal, it is essential to enlist the help of the parents and get them to change the modes of communication within the family, being careful not to sound accusatory or make the withdrawn child feel guilty. Such emotions are not helpful—they only prolong the problem or make the withdrawn child want to hide all the more. What Saitō sees as necessary are positive, concerted steps to move forward and help the many thousands of people suffering in silence. It is for that reason that he gives concrete steps to help families change their own behaviors at the same time that they are seeking help for themselves and their child. It would only be counterproductive to take the families of hikikomori children to task, saying that the culture within their family represents part of the problem.

Because the original Japanese version of this book was a *shinsho*, a paperback volume designed for a broad, nonspecialist audience, it does not contain the rigorous citations one would typically find in a medical journal or other research publications. At the end of the original Japanese book is a short bibliography of selected articles and monographs that Saitō mentions in the text, but this does not include citations for the works of the well-known American and European psychologists whom Saitō mentions in passing. As the translator, I have not bolstered the text with footnotes in order to boost its academic rigor. Instead, I have left in place the original system of citations, simple as it might be, adding to the bibliography only a few additional books that Saitō has mentioned with special frequency.

It is also worth noting that Saitō's many press appearances, especially in recent years, are not limited to the issue of withdrawal. He frequently appears in the press to comment on a host of issues about adolescent development, unemployment, media, and other factors affecting the lives of young people. Since 1998, the same year he first published this book in Japanese, he has been writing about other subjects as well. In *Bunmyaku-byō (The Disease of Context)*, Saitō applied the theories of Jacques Lacan, Gregory Bateson, and Humberto Maturana to his own clinical experience to provide a new look at Japanese culture (and youth subcultures in particular) in the context of the new postmodern flood of media and information, which Saitō saw as blurring the boundaries between the Lacanian realms of the real and the imaginary in sometimes startling and even productive ways. In *Shōjo-tachi no senreki (The Combat Service of Girls)*, a special issue of the serial *Pop Culture Critique* also published in 1998, Saitō provided a first look at the genealogy of the "beautiful fighting girl" *(sentō bishōjo)*, an archetypal figure in many manga and anime that has come to represent the object of erotic fascination for many male, heterosexual fans. Saitō developed this psychoanalytic foray into anime criticism in the 2000 volume *Sentō bishōjo no seishin bunseki*, which has been translated as *Beautiful Fighting Girl* by J. Keith Vincent and Dawn Lawson and also published by the University of Minnesota Press. There Saitō engages in an extended rereading of the history and (frequently mistaken) cultural assumptions about anime-loving subcultures and the influence of media on their imaginations. Although shaped by a sophisticated engagement with critical theorists from the West, this work is also grounded in common sense and his own down-to-earth observations gleaned from actual members of the subcultures under examination. This combination of theoretical sophistication, clinical observation, and careful practicality, especially when it comes to Japanese youth culture, is the hallmark of Saitō's work as a cultural theorist, and perhaps nowhere is that combination of factors on clearer display than in his work on social withdrawal.

As one final note to this introduction, I would like to share a personal anecdote. At the same time that I was giving this translation a final prepublication polish, one of the students studying at my university—an American student who was quite quiet but far above average in the classroom—confessed to me during my office hours that for some years, he had lived in a state of complete withdrawal in his own home, shell-shocked and unable to engage with the outside world. This condition had started for him in high school, and although he was a superior student, he dropped out for a time, maintaining only a minimal connection to society. Thanks to a loving family and some professional guidance, he recovered to the point that he completed a GED and came to university. Struck by this unexpected confession, I asked him if I could share the manuscript of this book with him. A couple of days later, he came to my office to tell me that he was overwhelmed when he read it—he was shocked at how similar his experiences were to the ones Saitō had described in this book.

For a long time the student had felt that he was alone, but the book offered proof that there were others like him in the world.

This experience offered one more piece of evidence to both me and Saitō, with whom I shared this story, that the experiences described in these pages are not entirely limited to Japan. Although the English-speaking world seems to be adopting the word *hikikomori*, rendering the word in transliterated Japanese instead of back-translating it into the original English word *withdrawal*, it is clearly not something found solely in Japan, and North American readers should not simply gawk at it as a "strange" phenomenon that seems only to happen elsewhere. It is my hope that this translation will spark debates in the English-speaking world, as the original book did in Japan, about the best ways to help all of the young people, regardless of their nationality or location, who are out there, hidden as they suffer in silence.

HIKIKOMORI

PREFACE TO THE ENGLISH EDITION

Fourteen years have gone by since this book was first published. Since then, there have been several gradual changes in Japan that have to do with hikikomori. Below I summarize some of the most important of those changes that have transpired during these fourteen years.

People are currently much more aware of the problem of social withdrawal than at the time when this book was first published. Nonetheless, there still is not yet enough treatment and support for the many people who need help. The word *hikikomori* is now known by everyone and used in ordinary conversation. This is true not just in Japan but internationally as well. The fact that the word *hikikomori* appeared in the *Oxford English Dictionary* in 2010 is evidence that the word has spread and is becoming increasingly recognizable outside Japan's borders; however, it is unfortunate that the definition incorrectly describes withdrawal as a specifically Japanese problem.

Currently, there are about 700,000 hikikomori in Japan. This is the number included in the newest, most up-to-date survey. In February 2010 the Japanese Cabinet Office conducted a survey of 5,000 people between the ages of fifteen and thirty-nine. In the results, the office estimates that there are 696,000 young hikikomori across the country who have been in a state of withdrawal in their homes for over six months. This is what the survey finds, but it is difficult to believe that all respondents answered accurately because there is so much shame associated with withdrawal. As a result, I believe that the number that I have put forth elsewhere—that there are 1 million people in a state of withdrawal in Japan—is probably still on target.

Early in 2000 two incidents transpired that brought an enormous amount of attention to the issue of withdrawal. The first was the January 2000 revelation that a thirty-seven-year-old hikikomori male in Kashiwazaki City, Niigata Prefecture, had kept a girl, who was nineteen years old at the time of her discovery, in captivity in his room for over nine years. The other incident took place in May, when a seventeen-year-old man hijacked a bus in Saga Prefecture. It was reported that both of these young men had histories of withdrawal, and so the media began talking about hikikomori as if they were a dangerous reserve army of potential criminals.

Of course, this reflects a severe misunderstanding. Withdrawal is an asocial condition, but the percentage of hikikomori who commit antisocial behavior is exceedingly small. There are no accurate statistics at the moment, but since those two events, there have been no major incidents involving hikikomori. If it is true that there is a population of 1 million hikikomori in our country, then that means that the proportion that turns to criminal behavior is, in fact, incredibly small.

In response to these two events, the Ministry of Health, Labor, and Welfare formed the "Research Group on Intervention in Activities to Preserve Psychological Health at the Local Level" and conducted a nationwide survey. The results of that survey were published in March 2001 in the preliminary version of the "Guidelines for Activities to Preserve Psychological Health at the Local Level, Especially in Regards to 'Social Withdrawal' among People in Their Tens and Twenties" (*Jū-dai, ni-jū-dai o chūshin to shita "shakai hikikomori" o meguru chiiki seishin hoken katsudō no gaidorain*).

These guidelines were distributed to psychology and healing centers throughout the country so that they could help people who needed to talk about withdrawal. In addition, there has been an increase in the number of municipalities that have taken up the issue and provided consultation centers for hikikomori. Big cities such as Sapporo, Yokohama, and Kobe have cooperated with private nonprofit organizations to start support services in a hybrid public–private model.

In 2003 NHK (Japan Broadcasting Corporation) started a year-long "Hikikomori Support Campaign." It created a web page to provide support, and the network prepared numerous special programs about hikikomori. That same year, the Ministry of Health, Labor, and Welfare published the finalized version of its guidelines.

The surge of media attention to the hikikomori problem helped pave the way for another development that took place soon after—the surge of media attention about NEETs that came in 2004. The word *NEET*, which began in Great Britain, is an acronym standing for "Not in Education, Employment, or Training," used to describe young people who are doing none of those things. This word was introduced as a way to talk about and support the employment of young men and women, but the people who came up with this term probably had no way to predict that it would indicate a pool of people so similar to hikikomori. As a result, people in Japan still frequently mix up the words *NEET* and *hikikomori*.

Recently, I have been paying more and more attention to how the issue of social withdrawal is connected with other social issues, including truancy, the prevalence of part-time workers who hop from job to job (called "freeters" in Japanese), and the high numbers of NEETs. All of these problems are interconnected in ways that influence one another. Because of this, I propose that we start thinking about these things in a more comprehensive way, using the concept of what I have called "the spectrum of asocial behavior" *(hishakaisei supekutoramu)*. If we use this broader outlook to look at these problems, then it becomes possible for us to understand how we might go about providing more comprehensive support, including medical help, public support, and employment assistance.

As research into withdrawal has progressed, it has become increasingly clear that withdrawal is not just a problem unique to Japan. For instance, withdrawal has become as much of a social problem in Korea as it is in Japan. According to Korean psychiatrists, there are approximately 300,000 hikikomori in South Korea.

The biggest difference between the situation in Japan and that in Korea is that people have pointed to online gaming addiction as a major reason for withdrawal in Korea. Korea has a system of conscription that requires young men to spend part of their youth in the military. The fact that Korea has a problem with withdrawal, even despite its system of compulsory military service, suggests that a policy of Spartan intervention will not be effective in treating withdrawal.

In 2006 Michael Zielenziger's book *Shutting out the Sun: How Japan Created Its Own Lost Generation* was published. This book, which was also translated into Japanese, was important in that it was the first major book to introduce the lives of hikikomori to the English-speaking world; however, his argument that the withdrawal of these hikikomori stems from a pathology in Japanese society is simply a misunderstanding. If withdrawal is not a problem found only in Japan, then it cannot be the case that it stems from some pathological characteristic of the Japanese people. It seems much more plausible that the explanation has more to do with the nature of the family and how young people deal with society. Below are a few of my thoughts on these points.

The problem of social withdrawal, along with the problem of youth homelessness, involves a failure of young people to engage with society. This problem exists everywhere in the world, in every country; however, in areas where there is a high percentage of young people living with their parents, there is a tendency for "social withdrawal" to increase, whereas in areas where there is a low percentage of young people living with their parents, there is a tendency toward greater numbers of homeless youths.

If one looks at the rates of parent–child cohabitation among developed nations, one finds that along with Japan and Korea, both Italy and Spain have cohabitation rates that exceed 70 percent. Italy is the one country in the European Union that has started to treat withdrawal as a social issue. I have heard from researchers in Spain that there is a similar problem there. On the other hand, in Britain, there are 250,000 homeless youths under the age of twenty-five.[1] According to a 2002 report from the Office of Juvenile Justice and Delinquency Prevention in the U.S. Department of Justice, there are over 1.6 million homeless and runaway youths in the United States—a number that has become infamous. In other words, the point is that in countries like the United States and Britain, the place for young people who find themselves unable to integrate into society is not in the home but on the streets.

How much sense does it make for us to argue about which society is more deeply pathological—a society that produces lots of hikikomori or a society that produces lots of homeless youths? If one is eager to talk in terms of social pathology, rather than talking just simply about "a pathology that is unique to Japan," it would probably make much more sense to analyze the patterns of various nations' pathologies and examine them side by side.

In 2009 the Japanese Ministry of Health, Labor, and Welfare formed another research group to conduct more investigations on withdrawal, and I participated as one of the members. The results of our investigation were published under the title *Guidelines for Evaluating and Supporting Hikikomori (Hikikomori no hyōka, shien ni kansuru gaidorain).*[2] This survey stated that people in withdrawal could be diagnosed with some kind of psychological disorder, but I am critical of this report. The reason is that most of the psychological symptoms that receive clinical treatment appear to be secondary symptoms accompanying the state of withdrawal; however, it is significant that this report indicated the relationship between withdrawal and developmental problems. This led me to realize that among the patients whom I am personally treating, about one in ten of my adult patients is suffering a developmental problem.

One thing that I have noticed is that hikikomori appear to be growing older. According to the survey, the average age of hikikomori now has reached 32.6 years of age. It appears that the reasons for this lie in extreme cases of long-term withdrawal that last for over twenty years, and in an increase in the number of cases of withdrawal that emerge after a person has found employment.

In the 2009 fiscal year the Ministry of Health, Labor, and Welfare formed a plan to counteract withdrawal *(hikikomori taisaku suishin jigyō),* and started proceeding with plans to create centers to support hikikomori at the local level that would be specifically dedicated to the problems of withdrawal and that would be the first line of defense. These were created in every prefecture and certain, designated cities. In the 2011 fiscal year the ministry also started an outreach-style program that centers on going into the household. The thing that I desire most from the current administration is for the government and municipalities to work to provide resources, and in doing so, to cooperate with private support organizations and non-profit organizations to construct a high-quality support network for the people who really need it.

The problem of withdrawal is already becoming so widespread and complicated that it is difficult for medical treatment alone to put it in check. The solutions cannot come only from the field of psychiatry. It will be best if specialists from different fields also become involved. At the very least, we will need the cooperation of specialists from education, psychology, medicine, welfare, career counseling, and life planning. I hope that through their cooperation, we can develop multilayered, multiple activities to support hikikomori and their recovery.

March 2012

INTRODUCTION

Have you heard stories like these?

> He's already thirty, but he doesn't work and just spends all his time hanging out at home.

> She hardly ever goes outside. Even when she's at home, she's always cooped up in her room.

> He keeps all the shutters closed, even during the day. For years, he's been living like there's no difference between night or day.

> On the rare occasions his parents suggest he get a job, he gets really angry, shouts, and even turns violent.

How do you feel about the people described above? Do any of the following statements reflect what you would have to say?

> It's a disgrace for an adult not to have a job and just to hang around doing nothing. Why on earth do some people let adults get away with that?

> Those obsessive *otaku* types are the ones who're the real problem. They're too quiet. Someone ought to check them into a mental hospital straight away.

> If a person doesn't work, he doesn't deserve to eat. If he doesn't feel like working, he ought to go to a boarding school or something and get some sense beaten into him.

It's the parent's fault. They must have raised their kid wrong. But I suppose if parents want to take care of their kids for their entire life, there's nothing anyone else can do about it.

In the end, it's our tax money that ends up taking care of apathetic, weak-kneed kids like that. We ought to be thinking about how to treat this like the social problem it is.

Sure enough. Those are the sorts of "reasonable opinions" you might expect to hear upstanding citizens say.

But what if there were tens of thousands of adolescents across the country who fit the descriptions I gave above? What if most of those young people were still unable to escape from their shut-in, withdrawn state even after being subjected to "reasonable opinions" over and over again? This is not just a hypothetical question.

Perhaps you are familiar with the words *shakaiteki hikikomori*—the Japanese translation of the English phrase *social withdrawal*. Originally, this was a psychological term that described a symptom seen in people suffering from a variety of psychological ailments.

In recent years, however, it has become increasingly clear that there are a significant number of adolescents in our country in a state of *shakaiteki hikikomori*, or *hikikomori* (withdrawal), as the phrase is sometimes shortened. According to one source, hundreds of thousands of people are living this state, and each year that number only increases. Of course, it is extremely difficult to determine the true numbers through surveys, and so we are still unable to ascertain the true scope of the problem accurately.

Nonetheless, based on empirical clinical experience, we psychologists are of the impression that the number of young people who fit the descriptions I have given above is gradually on the rise. I am not alone in this opinion. Numerous doctors have seen direct evidence of this.

As a psychiatrist, I have had a significant amount of contact over the last ten years or so with young people living a life of withdrawal. I have personally encountered probably over two hundred cases. This is just the number of cases where I actually interacted with the withdrawn individual for treatment. If I include people who just came for an initial consultation or people whom I just heard about in consultations, the number would be many times higher.

After graduating from the Medical College at Tsukuba University, I entered the research institute of Assistant Professor Inamura Hiroshi, who is now deceased. The first young men and women whom I encountered in his office were examples of socially withdrawn people. Dr. Inamura was a pioneer in the area.

Of course, we must not forget that even before Dr. Inamura's work, there were related problems, such as the "student apathy" and "retreat neurosis" that Kasahara Yomishi has described in his research. Kasahara provided us with extremely valuable pioneering studies of the lethargy that seems to affect such a disproportionately large number of young people in our country.

The problem of social withdrawal that I have been wrestling with, however, is even more complicated than what these two researchers have described. It is broader, and so it is difficult to get a clear look at the problem in its totality. Linked to the problem of social withdrawal are all sorts of problematic adolescent behaviors. Skipping school, domestic violence, thoughts of suicide, fear of others, obsessive actions, and so on—some of these, or sometimes even *all* of these, appear in some form within the "hikikomori" phenomenon.

It goes without saying that social withdrawal is a symptom, not the name of an illness. As I describe in more detail later, social withdrawal is a symptom that we often see accompanying various other mental conditions. There are many who feel social withdrawal should not be used as a diagnosis by medical psychologists; instead, psychologists should be providing diagnoses based on the other symptoms that accompany withdrawal.

In this book, I explain why I think we should pay attention to social withdrawal. Among the reasons is my belief that this is the simplest way to look at the problem, even as it opens up a path to more specialized treatments tailored to the individual case. In clinical situations it is most effective to look at problems in ways that are simple yet that yield a high possibility of practical treatment. In the case of a problem that cannot be entirely reduced to a single pathology, the way that we look at the problem is extremely important. The reason is that the problem can appear entirely different to us depending on how we go about looking at it.

If we are looking at withdrawal, can we really say that the number of people in withdrawal is actually on the rise? When I was in graduate school, I had a good deal of personal involvement with patients who were experiencing symptoms that we might classify as social withdrawal. After I finished graduate school and went to work as a psychiatrist, I have continued to perform psychiatric examinations in mental hospitals and clinics. After ten years of clinical treatment, I am now in a position where I am no longer new to the field, and I can make my own observations as I see them. The number of cases of withdrawal I have encountered over the last decade—two hundred or so—is probably more than the number encountered by the average psychiatrist of my generation. Still, one might argue, doesn't this high number simply indicate there are more people coming for *consultation* about social withdrawal? More about that shortly.

Of course, one should exercise caution in labeling social withdrawal as "pathological." I do, however, think that it is important to note, based on my own clinical experience, that as a patient's period of withdrawal from society grows longer, the easier it is for the patient to develop various pathologies. The problem of social withdrawal is not sufficiently understood. Is social withdrawal a mental illness or not? Is it a reflection of the problems of society? Is it something we should see as a product of family pathology? These debates have not yet really taken place. The fact that there is a real dearth of sources on the subject makes it difficult to tackle questions like these.

What motivated me to write this book was my sense that we may be facing a crisis because we simply do not have enough information. If society continues to fail to understand the problem, it will continue to treat it in an ad hoc way, and that will only delay the process of finding proper solutions. If we just think of withdrawal as a social illness or some sort of generational pathology, we will put off investigating the problem in any specific, concrete way. We cannot afford to wait. I was compelled to write this book by a sense of urgency, as well as a hope that my own clinical experience might be of some help. I suppose that in writing this, I also was trying to make sense of the many, often overwhelming clinical experiences I have had during the time I have spent in this field.

This book is divided into two parts: one having to do with theory and the other with practice. In the theory section, I discuss case studies and my own experience in treatment. I try to ask various theoretical questions about the nature of the problem, but I have made every effort to treat the subject in a way that will be accessible to mainstream readers. For that reason, I have kept my discussions relatively simple. In the section of this book dedicated to practice, I have attempted to write about concrete methods of treatment in ways that are as straightforward as possible. I do not mean to sound overbearing, but the practical advice in that section all comes out of my own personal experience in treating hikikomori cases. I hope that my advice will prove useful in real life and that it will also serve as an impetus to inspire further discussion.

PART I.
WHAT IS HAPPENING?

1 | WHAT IS SOCIAL WITHDRAWAL?

Tragedies of Indifference

In November 1996 a tragic incident took place: a middle school student took a bat and beat to death his father, who was an office worker in Tokyo. The father, whose life had been largely dedicated to work, could no longer stand his son's fits of violence in the household and had confronted him. The result was this tragedy. According to an article in the November 7 issue of the *Asahi Shinbun,* the student had been skipping school regularly for about a year and had been displaying violent behavior toward the other members of his family. As a result, his mother soon moved out of the house, leaving just the father and son to live alone. It was only a short time later that the father also found himself unable to withstand his son's fits of violence.

Does it make you uncomfortable that I have described such a tragic incident right away? Many similar incidents have taken place in recent years, and all of them are closely tied to the phenomenon of social withdrawal. I can say based on my own experience as a psychiatrist that it is not at all unusual for a person who feels cornered to strike back, sometimes causing unfortunate results. I cannot help but feel regret every time one of these tragic incidents takes place.

Clearly, there is a kind of ignorance that surrounds this type of crime. What makes this ignorance so hard to deal with is the fact that it is not limited to a simple lack of individual awareness. What we must deal with is a *structural* ignorance—an ignorance that is born out of social indifference. As long as this indifference continues, tragic incidents like the one I have described are likely to continue—that is to say, as long as we continue to fail to understand or pay attention to adolescent psychology and, above all else, the phenomenon of social withdrawal.

There may be some readers who do not agree with me and who think there has never been a time when we have paid *more* attention to adolescent psychology. On the surface, that is certainly true. Unfortunately, however, what people have tended to pay attention to is "adolescence as a social phenomenon." I will not go into the details here, except to point out that our society tends to pay attention to adolescence in relation to social customs, in relation to pathology, and in relation to certain incidents. On the other hand, we have continued to take little notice of how withdrawal prolongs adolescence.

Before I launch into a more detailed discussion, however, it is first necessary to answer a fundamental question. When people use the term *social withdrawal*, what are they talking about?

Four Case Studies

Sometimes when students skip school for whatever reason and that continues for an extended period of time, they are expelled from school and end up spending their time at home, remaining there well into even their twenties. Some of these former students who remain at home—perhaps even the majority—eventually reach a state of withdrawal in which they lose almost all connection to society whatsoever.

The words *shakaiteki hikikomori* that are used to refer to this state are a direct translation of the English words *social withdrawal*. In Japanese these words do not feel like a very idiomatic translation, but it is not hard to understand what it means—the *shakai* meaning "society" is used here to refer to relationships with other people in general. In other words, the term refers to the act of retreating from society and avoiding contact with all people other than one's own family. That is what is meant by *shakaiteki hikikomori*, or "social withdrawal."

Of course, skipping school is not the only thing that might lead to a state of withdrawal; however, in my own surveys and experience, it seems that the overwhelming number of cases begin when a student started skipping school and his or her period of absence grew ever longer and longer. I relate the results of my surveys in some detail later on, but for the moment, I will describe a handful of case studies.

Case Study 1: Twenty-Nine Years Old, Female

This woman has an introspective, serious personality, but she did not have any special troubles before graduating from high school. She studied dressmaking at a technical school and got a job at a hat shop, but she did not get along well with the other people at the shop. Half a year later, she quit and started spending most of her time in her room. She hardly went out to eat at all, and even though she used to be concerned about cleanliness, she stopped taking baths and showers. Even so, she managed to get a job at an office the following year, but her boss did not seem to like her, and so once again, she quit half a year later. After that, she spent her time at home making small handicrafts that she sold to relatives, helping out with the care of her sick grandfather, and so on.

One day, however, a relative made a disparaging remark about the poor quality of her handicrafts. The woman was extremely shocked by this and stopped making them all together. To make matters worse, her grandfather died soon after that, sending her into an even greater sense of despair. For some time, she lived in a continual state of absentmindedness, hardly doing a thing. Before long, she was living at home in a completely withdrawn state. She hardly comes out of her room and even avoids face-to-face confrontations with her own family. She spends most of the day in bed, and when night comes, she finally gets up and listens to music. This state of affairs has continued for about two years.

Case Study 2: Twenty-One Years Old, Male

When this young man was little, he was quite active and wanted to win at everything. Throughout high school, he was serious about sports and his studies, and without any trouble he was able to get into the university that was his first choice. Once at university, he joined the tennis club and attended class diligently. After the summer break of his freshman year, however, he suddenly stopped attending class. When his parents asked him why, he just responded that he had trouble in one particular class, and he did not get on well with his classmates.

After that, he gradually began to pay more attention to what people thought of him, and it became difficult for him to get on trains when he thought lots of people might be looking. When he was a sophomore in the middle of exams, he walked all the way home one day without using the trains at all. A psychologist diagnosed him as having anthropophobia, a debilitating fear of others. After that, he continued to go to university with the help of his parents, who accompanied him all the way to campus each day, but eventually he stopped going to his classrooms. He went to counseling for a month, which eased his anxiety somewhat. He also started a part-time job at the post office and attended a ceremony for his "coming-of-age" when he was twenty years old. Nonetheless, he still was not able to bring himself to enter his classrooms at school.

He tried going to the counseling office at the university, but he did not stick with it, and eventually he stopped attending school altogether. Since then, he has been spending his time at home. He has maintained a part-time job delivering newspapers, so he does leave home on his moped for that reason, and he also sometimes plays tennis. Most of the time, however, he stays at home. He has a relatively sunny disposition, but realistically, it does not seem like he can handle day-to-day life in quite the same way he once did.

Case Study 3: Thirty Years Old, Male

This man had no trouble in elementary and middle school, but during his freshman year of high school, he started skipping classes and throwing violent fits at home, hitting things and acting up when he did not get his way. He stopped attending school, but he was able to get a high school diploma through a correspondence course. After that, he started expressing strong opinions whenever anything was out of order in the house. He would get angry and throw a fit toward his mother if he found even the slightest speck of dirt. Unable to withstand the rages that now came almost daily, his mother moved out of the house, and before long, his father felt he had no choice but follow suit.

This state of separation has continued for six years. The man continues to live at home, while his parents live in a separate house they built recently. To this point, the man still does not have a job, and he continues to live alone, using the money his parents give him to support himself.

He sleeps during the day and is up all night. He keeps the windows and front door locked, and he communicates with his parents through written notes. He has no friends—in fact, no connection with other people whatsoever. Recently, he started demanding that his parents buy him a high-priced audio system. When his parents got one for him, he started complaining that it did not match his specifications exactly. His parents responded, "If you want it, buy it yourself," but that sent him into a terrifying rage. He started demanding that his parents pay him a lot of money as a "fine," and he sent them threatening letters that said he was going to kill them.

Case Study 4: Twenty-Nine Years Old, Male

This man was not especially strong-willed to begin with. There was a point in middle school when he wanted to quit a club he was in, but he could not bring himself to tell the other members or the leader of the club; instead, he asked his father to make excuses for his absence. Eventually, he did quit without warning. There were times in high school when he would get drunk and behave badly.

After graduating from college, he got a job in a company in his hometown, but he quit within a month. He also quit his next job within half a year. Since then, he has moved from job to job several times, but none of them has ever lasted more than a few months. Also, each time he has quit, he has not told anyone. Instead, he just stopped showing up to work or disappeared. After leaving work, he has lived at home, spending his time cooped up indoors.

One May when he was twenty-six, he slashed his wrists, perhaps because this lifestyle was so difficult for him to bear. He started seeing a psychiatrist after his failed attempt at suicide. He behaved violently toward his family at first, but with the help of his doctor, he has lived in a relatively calm state through the present day, yet he continues to live cooped up at home, doing nothing.

This Phenomenon Is Not a Temporary "Fad"

The four "case studies" I have just presented are semifictitious constructions that combine the stories of patients whom I have treated directly and others I have not. As a general rule, I try to protect the privacy of my patients and do not divulge the details of their cases in books I write for a general audience, so I ask for your indulgence on this point. I can say with conviction, however, that withdrawal takes very different forms in each particular case. Still, a number of similarities seem to recur.

A large number of cases involve people who are introverted to begin with—often the types who are considered "good" boys and girls and who "don't require too much looking after." Most do not go through a rebellious phase, and in fact, many have an almost overly methodical quality to their personality that can develop into obsessive-compulsive disorder, such as the obsession for checking meaningless details. This does not mean, however, that all children who shut themselves away display these sorts of tendencies. It is not unusual to find seemingly "ordinary" people who happen to hit a stumbling block in life, become so depressed that their personality seems to change altogether, and shut themselves away from society. Some of these people were outgoing through middle school; some even served as their class representatives at school. Some were good at sports through high school and were able to express their opinions without any trouble. I think it is a special characteristic of hikikomori cases that there is not one fixed personality trait that manifests itself in every single case.

One particular trait, however, is clear. The overwhelming majority of hikikomori cases involve men. Moreover, when I looked at where those men fall in the family birth order, my surveys showed that a large number are oldest sons. I am not saying that there are no cases involving women, but generally, when women begin to withdraw from society, their behavior tends not to last for an extended period of time. In addition, most hikikomori cases I have seen have come from well-educated parents who are middle class or above. It is not uncommon to find a father who works hard and cares little about child rearing, and an overbearing mother. It is not uncommon that there are many people around them, perhaps members of the immediate family or relatives, who are distinguished and hard-working, thus placing increased psychological pressure on the person in withdrawal.

Once people enter into a state of withdrawal, they hardly go outside; instead, they sleep during the day and are active at night, avoid their families, and tend to coop themselves up in their own rooms. Their sense of self-pride, concerns about their appearance, and the deteriorating relationship with their own family cause them concern and mental discord, sometimes even leading to angry, violent fits or even attempted suicide. In some cases, hikikomori cases display symptoms such as obsessive-compulsive disorder or anthropophobia. These symptoms only prolong the state of withdrawal even further and create a vicious circle that is increasingly difficult to escape from.

In this way, the stubborn state of apathy and of withdrawal grows even longer. The period of withdrawal can last from a few months to years. One of the longest cases I have seen involved a young man who shut himself away for well over a decade.

As the symptoms progress and extend over an increasingly long period of time, it simply seems to others that the person is being lazy and acting lethargic, but often, there are deep conflicts and strong, fretful feelings hidden below the surface. As evidence, one can see that the majority of people in withdrawal do not experience boredom, even though they spend their days not doing anything. Their minds appear to be occupied, not giving them the psychological room to feel bored.

There are a few unfortunate, overlapping factors that make the issue of social withdrawal so problematic. The first problem is that even though it is possible to prevent and treat it, there are hardly any facilities designed to do so. Families trying to deal with this problem typically have nowhere to turn to but a psychiatrist; however, psychiatrists tend to be halfhearted in dealing with the problem. In the next chapter I discuss at length the opinions of psychiatrists in Japan, but for the time being, let me just say that the methods of dealing with the issue lag significantly behind the problem itself. The biggest reason we will be in trouble if we do not change anything is that the hikikomori state almost never naturally resolves itself on its own. As I explain later, one cannot explain the problem of social withdrawal as merely the product of individual pathology. It is absolutely necessary to understand social withdrawal as a pathological system that involves both society and the family as well. Psychiatrists should make efforts to alleviate this pathological system, but at the moment, the psychiatric world has not yet arrived at a fixed consensus about how to do that.

Social withdrawal is not just some sort of temporary "fad" that will pass away. It is not something we can easily classify as "such and such syndrome." It has been eleven years since I first started dealing with this subject, but during that time, there has been no sign that the number of cases will decrease. The numbers of cases are not exploding, but there is certainly no decrease either. If anything, there has been a small but steady increase in the number of hikikomori cases I have seen. In fact, I think we should be even more concerned about this issue than if it were some sort of "syndrome" going through society. Why? Let us suppose for a moment that the numbers of new hikikomori cases *were* on the decrease. If we fail to change in the way we treat or counsel those patients in withdrawal, we would still see an *increase* in the absolute number of people in withdrawal. The reason is that they do not get better on their own and simply end up shutting themselves away for longer and longer periods of time.

How should we psychiatrists respond? In this book, I speak frankly about the things I have experienced personally, the things I have thought, and the things I do in working with hikikomori patients. I hope that this book will spark further debate on this important issue.

The Definition of "Social Withdrawal"

Before going on to speak about problems involved with withdrawing from society, I think it is important to define up front the words *social withdrawal*, which I use throughout this book. For the purposes of this book, I define social withdrawal as follows.

> A state that has become a problem by the late twenties, that involves cooping oneself up in one's own home and not participating in society for six months or longer, but that does not seem to have another psychological problem as its principal source.

Perhaps the words *by the late twenties* is opening the door a bit too wide. If one were to change these to read *by the early twenties*, that would still cover most of the cases I have dealt with. There are two reasons that I have included an age in this definition. One reason is that I want to stress this problem is related to the problems of adolescence. It is commonly accepted among clinical psychologists who deal with large numbers of adolescents that young people nowadays do not become a full adult at age twenty; they become adults at age thirty. Based on actual observations, psychiatrists seem to agree that the adolescent mind-set continues more or less until around the time a person turns thirty. If a person begins to live a life of withdrawal after the age of thirty, then one should probably assume that there is some other cause. Personally, however, I have never encountered such a case.

The *six months or longer* in my definition is a unit of time commonly used in the American Psychiatric Association's *DSM-IV (Diagnostic and Statistical Manual of Mental Disorders, Fourth Edition)* and other books to talk about the length of psychological symptoms. I could have chosen other units of time, such as three months or a year, but there are two reasons that I did not. First, if I define the unit of time as less than six months, I might provoke families to engage in excessive countermeasures. It is not at all uncommon that young people withdraw and coop themselves up for a relatively short time to take some time off from the world and engage in necessary recuperation. I think that in those situations, it makes more sense to let young people take their time and rest rather than press them into treatment. Conversely, if I identify the period in the definition as longer than six months (e.g., "one year"), treatment will come too late. If the withdrawn state continues for more than six months, then I think it is advisable for the family to get their child in withdrawal some treatment.

The last portion about not arising as the result of some other psychological affliction probably does not need any special explanation. Only after we eliminate the possibility of other psychological ailments with similar symptoms can we begin to think seriously about how to deal with this issue and treat it. In the next chapter, I explain in detail the various psychological afflictions that can be used as indicators of a state of social withdrawal.

Problems of Symptoms and Diagnosis

Even though it is easy to say "social withdrawal" in a single breath, there are various, different states that could be included under this rubric. As I explain later, when confronted with the question of how to diagnose hikikomori cases, a majority of psychiatrists tend to diagnose the symptoms that accompany the withdrawn state. In other words, they will diagnose withdrawn patients who have a strong fear of other people as having "anthropophobia," or withdrawn patients who display strong obsessive tendencies as having "obsessive-compulsive disorder," and so on. I believe those psychiatrists are acting on their best judgment, so I cannot say that they are entirely wrong, but I also do not agree with them entirely either. Why not?

When a person who has a cold goes to see a doctor, he or she has a number of *symptoms,* such as a cough, sore throat, headache, fever, and so on. Those manifest themselves as a *state*—having "a fever of 100.4 degrees Fahrenheit, a cough that won't let up, and heaviness in the head that won't go away." As a result, one *diagnosis* that might come out of this is that the patient has "upper respiratory inflammation." If one tries to diagnose social withdrawal based on its symptoms, one will not end up with a proper "diagnosis" like the "upper respiratory inflammation" I have just described. Instead, one will end up with so-called diagnoses that are the equivalent of "coughing syndrome" or "headache syndrome"—diagnoses that do not really address the full complexity and underlying cause of the problem.

The various symptoms that accompany social withdrawal are sometimes secondary. In other words, first, there is a state of withdrawal from society, and as that state continues, it gives rise to various other symptoms. I believe that it is of crucial importance that we think of the hikikomori state as a primary symptom. There are several reasons for this.

First, the most continuous, stable, single symptom is the withdrawal from society itself. To put it conversely, in most cases, the various other symptoms that accompany the state of withdrawal ebb and flow along with the process of withdrawal itself. To give an example, I have seen cases in which patients experienced delusions that their body had an odor (bromidrophobia) at the beginning of their period of withdrawal. As the withdrawal continued, however, those symptoms lessened, and the patient began to experience paranoid delusions or obsessive compulsions. If one were to diagnose those cases based on symptoms alone, then the diagnosis would change every time the symptoms did, too. The result would be a diagnosis that does not reflect real life.

It is also important to consider social withdrawal as a major factor leading to various other symptoms. For instance, the anthropophobic fear of others that accompanies withdrawal often grows worse as the period of withdrawal increases. In such situations, it is highly possible that anthropophobia is a secondary symptom or, at the very least, is exacerbated by the state of withdrawal. It is only natural that people grow increasingly more frightened of interacting with others the longer they live without interaction. As a result, they fall into a vicious circle, with their state of withdrawal growing ever deeper.

A great deal of clinical experience backs up what I have just said about certain symptoms being secondary. For instance, when a patient is hospitalized, sometimes symptoms of neurosis that had been affecting a patient quite badly suddenly disappear as a result of the change in environment. Even symptoms such as anthropophobia, which is ordinarily difficult to treat without hospitalization, can sometimes disappear without a trace.

That being the case, when treating hikikomori, there is a tendency to pay attention to individual symptoms, especially the burden of worry that the withdrawn state causes within the patient. Indeed, it would be difficult to proceed with treatment *without* dealing with the feelings of inferiority and the concern that withdrawal causes. Still, I believe that if we are trying to think about practical ways to approach the issue as psychiatrists, we should think about "social withdrawal" first, and then grapple with diagnosis and treatment on that basis.

A Special Pattern of Adolescent Conflict

Social withdrawal is a problem that originates in the mind. In other words, we must think of it as being different from other afflictions and mental illnesses that arise as a result of the structure of the brain itself.

Also, social withdrawal is deeply rooted in an adolescent mind-set, regardless of what age the person actually happens to be. In other words, one can look at social withdrawal as arising from the failure to mature as one travels along the path of character development. When most people talk about "adolescence," they typically imagine it to mean the time from around twelve to eighteen years of age, or to put it another way, the period of time in which the framework for the personality is formed and the body undergoes sexual maturation. I used the rather unwieldy phrase "framework for the personality," but I suppose that you could simply use the words "personality" as well. As Harry Stack Sullivan and others have pointed out, in the process of growing, the tendencies of the personality are fairly well set by the late years of elementary school and are temporarily stabilized; as the child develops secondary sex characteristics, he or she experiences various conflicts, which become the source of many adolescent anxieties. It is no exaggeration to say that sexual maturation is the most important psychological issue between adolescence and early adulthood.

In hikikomori cases, the patterns of personal conflict usual in adolescence continue over many years. This statement is grounded in the following reasons.

• Social withdrawal is often accompanied by symptoms closely related to the adolescent mind-set, such as skipping school, throwing violent fits at home, obsessive-compulsive disorder, and fear of others.

• As the length of the period of withdrawal increases, many modes of thought and self-involvement characteristic of adolescence appear, including narrowness of vision and inflexibility.

• The person in withdrawal is not able to assess his or her own situation objectively and therefore refuses treatment in most cases.

• Even in hikikomori cases that continue over a long period of time, chronic symptoms tend not to stabilize; instead, there is a continuous state of mental conflict that gives rise to more mental conflict, as if new wounds are constantly opening.

- Hikikomori cases are often best treated through clinical treatments that support the psychological growth of the person in withdrawal as well as adjustments to the environment, including the environment provided by the family.

In conjunction with these points, let's look in more detail at the special characteristics and symptoms associated with social withdrawal.

2 | THE SYMPTOMS AND DEVELOPMENT
OF SOCIAL WITHDRAWAL

Statistical Surveys of Social Withdrawal

I hope that in the last chapter, I was able to provide a rough picture of what social withdrawal looks like. In this chapter I intend to give readers get a clearer understanding by presenting the results of a survey conducted in 1989. Before launching into the results, however, I will first describe the survey itself.

This survey involved patients who during the six years between January 1983 and December 1988 received treatment in the offices affiliated with the research institute to which I belong. To be a subject, the patients had to meet the following criteria.

- Did not have an underlying disease such as schizophrenia (see later section), manic-depressive disorder, or an organic psychosis.

- Had already experienced three months or more of lethargy and withdrawal by the time of their earliest consultation.

- Had been receiving continuous treatment for at least six months as of June 1989.

- Had come to the clinic at least five times (this criterion was included because many consultations involve only the parents alone).

- Had enough documentation to warrant giving them the survey questionnaire.

There were eighty patients who met these conditions (sixty-six men, fourteen women). At the time of their earliest consultations, their ages ranged from 12 to 34 years old. The average age was 19.6 years old. At the time of the survey, their ages ranged from 13 to 37, with an average age of 21.8. The survey was carried out with this patient sample by giving a survey questionnaire that I and my colleagues had created. As a general rule, I entrusted the individual physicians in charge with the surveys, and the results were analyzed statistically with computers.

Our survey turned up the following results, which one might use to help understand the major characteristics of social withdrawal.

- The average length of time for the period of withdrawal, according to the survey, was thirty-nine months (three years and three months).

- Men are overwhelmingly more likely to experience withdrawal.

- The percentage of eldest sons is especially high.

- The average age at which the problem first arose was 15.5 years old.

- The most common trigger initiating the withdrawal was "skipping school," seen in 68.8 percent of the cases.

- After the problem began, a long period of time elapsed before the patient came to seek counseling at a treatment facility.

- The families are middle class or above, and there were relatively few families where the parents were divorced or living apart because of work.

Each of these results requires further investigation, but I save that for later. For the moment, I am simply trying to create an overall, factually based picture of this group of patients, since under ordinary circumstances it is quite hard to get an accurate picture of what the lives of people in withdrawal are like.

Next, based on the results of the same survey, I discuss the symptoms that accompany social withdrawal. I do not limit myself to what people recognize as psychological symptoms; instead, I try to give a comprehensive survey of the various kinds of abnormal states that might arise as a person enters and progresses through an extended period of withdrawal.

Of course, there are certain symptoms (such as compulsive over-eating or anorexia) that should be given their own separate treatment. The needs depend on the symptoms. What I discuss below are those symptoms that I believe to arise as secondary symptoms out of the state of social withdrawal. I have included symptoms here even if I believe that there is even the slightest possibility they are prompted by the state of withdrawal itself.

Listlessness and Social Withdrawal

First, to what extent is a general state of listlessness a part of the ex-perience of withdrawal? According to the results of the 1989 survey, 67 percent of respondents said that at the time that they were first seen by a doctor, they "hardly ever went outside, or occasionally went only as far as their own neighborhood." Also, at the time of the survey, the average length of time for the period of withdrawal was thirty-nine months, but the periods of withdrawal varied a good deal de-pending on the person.

Currently, the patients whom I am treating are almost all twenty years or older. As I explain later, many cases started when the patient began skipping school. If one considers that fact, it is only natural that many of these patients have already been in a state of withdrawal for a few years or more. Hardly any of the patients have much work experi-ence beyond a part-time job.

Judging from these results, is it correct simply to call hikikomori "lazy"? To understand their feelings, one should try to imagine the circumstances that caused them to feel forced to continue this life behind closed doors doing nothing for years. A withdrawn lifestyle typically involves a great deal of anguish. If individuals do *not* experi-ence anguish or discomfort in living this way, then they are the ones we should really be worried about. Those who do not feel any anguish living a life of withdrawal for over a year should be checked to see if they are experiencing some other kind of mental illness.

The majority of hikikomori cases do not choose on their own to keep living that way just because they want to. They want more than anyone else to escape from their withdrawn situation, but they simply are not able to do so.

The Relationship with Skipping School

As I mentioned briefly before, many people are under the general impression that skipping school is often the thing that most often triggers a life of social withdrawal. Indeed, in our survey, we found that "not attending school" was the most common answer when we asked for the event that initiated the withdrawn state.[1] Are skipping school and the withdrawal necessarily sequential?

If I were to answer yes, this would only be a source of new anxiety for families who currently happen to have children who do not always attend school regularly. Will children who skip school be unable to live good lives as productive members of society? There are many families who have this fear.

Indeed, it does seem that skipping school triggered the entry into a withdrawn state for many people. But to say that skipping school represents the *cause* for withdrawal, one would have to do more surveys, this time focusing on children who skip school to gauge what percentage end up in a state of social withdrawal.

A lot of data has been collected on this question, for instance, studies that deal with the prognosis for students who refuse to go to school. After a look at the results of those studies, my impression is that if we look at all the students who have stopped attending school, we would find very few who ended up in social withdrawal. The facts are that a majority of the people who play hooky seem to be able to avoid falling into a long, drawn-out period at home. As a result, there is no need to assume that not going to school will necessarily lead to social withdrawal.

Nonetheless, it is also a clinical fact that there *is* a certain percentage of people who do skip school and do end up in a severe state of withdrawal. If we ignore that fact, we might fail to handle the issue in appropriate ways.

On the one hand, it is not necessary to overproblematize skipping school. On the other, I am not saying that we should defend the skipping of school by taking an attitude that seems to romanticize it altogether—there is no need to say, for instance, "There's almost no way that decent, sensitive kids won't skip school, given the modern educational system. Kids are in their natural element when they're not in school." That attitude gives too much credit to the delinquent student and can cause adults to become unresponsive. The issue of school attendance is also tangled up in thorny issues about quality of life, so there is a tendency to give up too quickly on clinical advice that might prove helpful. We can see this attitude in the slogan "Not going to school is not an illness."[2] To sum up, I am not trying to say that all students who play hooky should undergo clinical treatment, but it is a fact that a certain percentage of students skipping school could be helped by attending to their needs in a clinical fashion. Personally, I agree that there is some truth in the slogan "Not going to school is not an illness," but I feel strongly that we should be sure not to fail *altogether* to respond to students who skip school.

Most people already know someone in their close circle of friends and acquaintances who has some experience with a person who has stopped attending school. Certain children who do skip school for a period of time do end up taking college entrance exams and deciding what path in life they would like to take, but there are others who just end up hiding themselves away. If we romanticize truancy, I feel as if we might be discriminating against those children in another way—allowing some to slip through the cracks. In the shadows of the "elite" kids who skip school—those students who *do* manage to pull themselves up by the bootstraps and participate in society—there seems to be a large number of kids who start out skipping school, then find themselves unable to go out in society, even though they feel constant irritation at themselves because of their social paralysis.

Let me make an analogy. If we compare skipping school to a disease, it would probably be something on the level of a cold, but social withdrawal would be more like pneumonia or tuberculosis. This analogy gets at both the range of the "ailments" and the level of listlessness involved in each. I believe that in the way society relates to it, social withdrawal is in much the same position as tuberculosis was before the invention of antibiotics.

So as not to be misunderstood, let me explain this analogy in a little more detail.

1. One becomes more prone to both social withdrawal and tuberculosis (i.e., as tuberculosis manifested itself before antibiotics) when one experiences a prolonged state of exhaustion, shock, or fatigue.

2. Both require an adjustment to the environment and an approach that involves taking care of the health generally, rather than a specific course of treatment. (Of course, for tuberculosis, this changed with the discovery of antibiotics.)

3. In terms of the way they are treated by society, unwarranted misunderstandings and prejudice sometimes affect the way both are handled.

4. Both involve the family to a fairly great degree. One major cause for this is the reason listed in point 3.

5. Patients are constantly criticized by society because patients have the appearance of being able to get a job when, in reality, they are not.

If this analogy is correct, then it would be nice if it provided some hints about treatment or alleviating the symptoms. However, since social withdrawal is fundamentally a problem having to do with the mind, it seems unlikely that some sure-fire cure will cure social withdrawal, as antibiotics did for tuberculosis.

In the past, people used stronger language—"the refusal to go to school" (tōkō kyohi)—to describe what we now call "nonattendance at school" (futōkō), and people treated it as a social problem. However, given that the numbers of such students have risen to over one hundred thousand nationwide (according to the Fundamental Survey of Schools conducted by the Ministry of Education in 1996) and that nonattendance at school has become a part of daily life, the theory that this tendency represents a "sickness" loses its explanatory power. The rise in numbers, which runs contrary to the decline in the total number of school-aged people because of low birthrates, seems to prove that nonattendance at school is a direct reflection of some social pathology. If it were some sort of regular psychological ailment, then we would not likely find such a dramatic increase in numbers. On the other hand, as we know from the fact that certain psychological symptoms decrease in times of war, it is not necessarily the case that social pathology is reflected directly in individual psychological ailments. Later on, I talk at greater length about what sorts of "sickness" might be "reflected" in social withdrawal.

In our survey, nearly 90 percent of our hikikomori patients went through a period of skipping school. There is no doubt that this number is quite high; however, as I explained before, it is a mistake simply to assume that not attending school necessarily leads to social withdrawal. A significant number of people who do play truant for a while end up participating in society in some fashion—returning to school, getting a job, and so on. Of course, it is also wrong to say that there is no connection whatsoever between skipping school and social withdrawal—it is clear as day that a certain portion of the people who stop attending school end up in an extended period of truancy and eventually withdraw from society.

The expression *nonattendance at school* covers lots of territory; it is used to describe various different situations, since there can be many reasons for a student to stop going to school. It is careless to bundle all of those different situations together and treat them in exactly the same way, just as it is careless to bundle together all cases of social withdrawal and treat them in exactly the same way. At the same time, however, we cannot ignore that there is a noticeable overlap between people suffering from that group of symptoms associated with social withdrawal and those people who are truant.

According to our survey, among the people who did stop attending school for a while, 86 percent skipped school continuously for three months or more. From this fact, it seems possible to conjecture that there are many cases in which the period of truancy grew longer, leading the person into a state of withdrawal. One characteristic of social withdrawal is that relatively few patients had experienced a long period of social participation in the form of a job or other similar activities that extended over a lengthy period of time. One could explain this by describing social withdrawal as a form of "immaturity." The withdrawn state always involves problems carried over from adolescence. What I am trying to say is that after one has achieved a high level of social maturation, then it is rare for a person to slip into a state of social withdrawal. At least, I do not know of any such cases.

Fear of Others

One of the most common psychological symptoms that one finds in people who are in a state of social withdrawal is an aversion or fear of others (anthropophobia); however, the simplistic equation "social withdrawal equals difficulty interacting with other people" is not correct, although people sometimes make that assumption. In general, it is not uncommon for people in withdrawal to be able to interact with others with relative ease, provided those interactions are limited to certain individuals or situations. (Conversely, even when a person is entirely healthy, there are probably very few individuals who can interact with *anybody* in *all* situations without experiencing some sort of difficulty somewhere along the road.)

What is important to note here is that, when the period of social withdrawal is prolonged, it becomes increasingly difficult for the person who is withdrawing to interact with others. Our survey found that 41 percent of the respondents said they had either one or no friends at all at the time of the questionnaire. Among the people who said that they did have some friends, only 23 percent said they were in frequent contact with those friends or did things with them. One should probably do another study to compare these numbers with the ordinary population, but just by looking at these numbers, it is obvious that most people in withdrawal live in a state of impoverished human relations. Also, at the time of the survey, 78 percent of respondents said that they had no experience with the opposite sex. When one considers that the average age of the respondents was twenty-two years old, these responses seem to hint at a relative lack of experience with other people.

What about the actual numbers of people actually experiencing "fear of others"? If one includes the respondents who had experienced the fear that they were omitting a body odor (bromidrophobia), the fear of blushing in front of others (erythrophobia), and symptoms of the fear of others (anthropophobia), the number comes to 67 percent.

There were many different ways in which people expressed "symptoms of the fear of others." Even among those respondents who had a relatively light degree of withdrawal and who did not have a very strong aversion to going outside, a significant number said they were "concerned about looks from neighbors." A number of people expressed relatively specialized situations, such as "nervousness and anxiety on seeing someone in uniform" or being "unable to approach an older person." There was also a young man in his twenties who had been the victim of severe bullying when he was in middle school and who expressed "fear of groups of people in school uniforms" on more than one response. In cases like this when there is a combination of fear and the possibility of provocation, even the slightest thing can set off a person and make him or her ready for conflict.

In addition, there were respondents who said, "I cannot get on a train or bus because I am concerned about other people looking at me." There were many others who said they had a strong aversion to other people entering their homes so they would hide or do other things when people came to visit. There were even respondents who would refuse to answer the telephone.

Even among the respondents able to participate in society to a certain degree, there were some who said they were unable to relax around others, even if those others were of a limited group. They often blamed themselves, saying things like "When I'm around others, I just wreck the mood" or "I don't have much to talk about so I'm a killjoy when I'm in the middle of a group of people." In more severe situations, one finds symptoms of bromidrophobia, as respondents say things like "I'm really concerned I've got bad body odor," or the fear of one's own gaze, as respondents say things like "I'm worried I'll hurt someone since my glance is so sharp."[3]

One also often sees symptoms of dismorphophobia, the fear that one's own appearance is ugly, even though in most cases outsiders probably would not agree. There are cases where people in withdrawal become so hung up on their unique features that they stop interacting with others, saying things like "my nose is crooked," "my hair is too thin," "I've got too many zits," or "I'm too fat."

Until fairly recently, specialists seem to have thought the fear of blushing (erythrophobia) was a symptom that represented a broader fear of interaction with others (anthropophobia), but it is now said that this symptom is on the decline. My impression seems to support this; I seem to have encountered few people who experience this fear, but the thing that strikes me as taking its place is dismorphophobia. Almost all of the patients in withdrawal who complain their appearance is too ugly to interact with others end up going to see cosmetic surgeons. Insurance does not cover elective surgery, so they run up against the barrier of the high price tag, and so not all of them have cosmetic surgery in the end. There are, however, hikikomori patients who force their parents to cough up the money and go through with it.

Some readers might assume that dismorphophobic hikikomori who do have surgery find themselves satisfied and are able to leave their state of withdrawal right away; however, that is not the way these symptoms work, and indeed, that is what makes them so hard to treat. In most situations, the results of the surgery do not satisfy the patients. Even if they make a claim against the cosmetic surgeon, the situation remains unsettled, and they end up withdrawing from the world even further.

Obsessive-Compulsive Disorder

Obsessive-compulsive disorder refers to a strong fixation that involves engaging in certain meaningless acts or thoughts. It is relatively close to the image we have of people who are overly methodical. For instance, a person with obsessive-compulsive disorder might go to check whether the gas is off over and over even though he knows it is probably off; he might not feel at ease unless the edges of all the books or notebooks are lined up perfectly, or he might wash his hands over and over after coming in from outside.

Another symptom can be seen in people who cannot help but think of a certain image or phrase over and over again. These are called obsessions. There are many people who, when confronted with a person of good standing, cannot help but imagine that person doing something obscene. One can think of an obsession as something like that, except much more dramatic.

It sometimes happens that obsessive-compulsive tendencies manifest themselves in conjunction with the withdrawn state. In fact, my impression is that the kinds of obsessive-compulsive behaviors I have just described are relatively common in hikikomori cases. In our survey, 53 percent of the respondents also experienced "symptoms of obsessive-compulsive disorder." My personal impression is that the longer the period of withdrawal, the more likely the patient is to experience obsessive-compulsive symptoms. It does not seem that there are many cases in which hikikomori enter into a withdrawn state because of their obsessive-compulsive behaviors; rather, those behaviors usually developed as secondary traits after going into withdrawal. For instance, there have been cases when patients who were in an extended period of social withdrawal were unable to stop their obsessive-compulsive behaviors and were hospitalized, but immediately afterward, the symptoms of obsessive-compulsive behavior disappeared. This leads me to believe that the obsessive-compulsive symptoms associated with withdrawal are slightly different than what one finds in the obsessive-compulsive nervous disorder itself.

Strong obsessive-compulsive behaviors are often accompanied by violent fits. In particular, the type of behavior Narita Yoshihiro has called the "dragging-in pattern" (makikomi-gata) tends to exhaust both the hikikomori themselves and their families, because they are trying to involve their parents with their obsessive-compulsive behaviors. I encountered one case in which a withdrawn patient would ask his mother over and over if she had touched his things, and if she could not respond to his satisfaction, then he would start all over, rephrasing the question over and over in different ways. I have also encountered cases in which a hikikomori patient was hung up on cleanliness and could not stop himself from washing his hands over and over so often that he was rubbing his own skin away. There was another hikikomori patient who could not touch doorknobs or television remote controls directly and instead would grab these things through the safety of a tissue. I have also known of a few rather severe cases in which the patient could not stand the saliva building up in his mouth and would spit it out inside the house, or the patient could not help but urinate inside his room. Obsessive-compulsive behaviors that involve repeated confirmation often involve the mother, and it is not uncommon that the patient will break out into a dramatic rage if the mother refuses to respond or makes even a slight refusal.

Even when symptoms are not so extreme, one frequently finds relatively mild cases of obsessive-compulsive behaviors among patients in withdrawal. For instance, the patients might be extremely fastidious about the time at which they eat and take their baths, and even a small delay of a few minutes could send them into a temper tantrum. Another possibility is that they might demand that the paths they use to walk around inside the house are always neat and tidy.

It may seem that most people in withdrawal are not concerned with bodily hygiene, but their appearance is often a product of the fact that they are *overly* concerned about it. For instance, it is quite common that when hikikomori get into the bathtub, they clean themselves with such meticulous care that the bath ends up taking hours. For people who have those symptoms, just getting into the bath leaves them completely exhausted; therefore, they end up getting in only on rare occasions.

It is also common that people in withdrawal are preoccupied with the cleanliness of other people in their family, but their own rooms are full of things, perhaps even garbage. As in the case with the bathing that I mentioned before, when they start to clean up their room, they are such perfectionists that they start over and over again, hitting a roadblock each time and getting easily frustrated. It is quite common that hikikomori are so overly fond of order that, ironically, they end up becoming disorderly or living in messy, unclean rooms.

Insomnia and Reversal of Night and Day

Both of these are "symptoms" that one sees in most cases of social withdrawal. According to the survey, 68 percent of the respondents required sleeping medicine, at least temporarily, for insomnia. Eighty-one percent of the respondents said that they had a tendency to reverse their sleeping hours, thus reversing night and day. It seems fair to say that these symptoms also arose as a result of the withdrawn state. It seems that there are both physiological and psychological reasons for these symptoms.

Let's address the physiological reasons first. When the human body is active during the day, the sympathetic nervous system predominates, but when sleeping, the body switches over to the parasympathetic nervous system. In other words, our sympathetic nerves are more active when we are in stressful situations, but when we are in a relaxed state, our parasympathetic nervous system is in greater control. People who are in withdrawal, however, tend to spend their waking hours without doing much of anything and just watching television, so the natural stress–relax modulation of the body tends to become fuzzy. For that reason, the balance of the autonomic nerves tends to break down, and one begins to see various symptoms appearing in the body. The most representative ones are insomnia and the tendency to reverse day and night.

There is another reason it is easy to break the ordinary cycle in which nighttime sleep cancels out the tension and exhaustion of the daytime. The human body is equipped with an internal clock that governs daily rhythms, but the thing that adjusts that internal clock is sunlight. Exposure to sunlight during the day maintains the ordinary cycles of the internal clock. By withdrawing from society, there is an extreme decrease in the exposure to sunlight, and this also helps spur the tendency to reverse day and night.

Moreover, there are psychological reasons why people reverse day and night. I explain this in more detail later, but people in withdrawal experience extreme feelings of inferiority as a result of their situation. During the daytime when everyone is out doing their activities, people in withdrawal cannot help but feel a strong inferiority complex, that something is wrong with them. In other words, they can hardly stand the anguish of being awake and spending another pointless day. For that reason, they end up spending more time awake at night, and the trend toward insomnia that I described earlier ends up getting worse. Over time, their waking hours gradually slip later and later, until they are the reverse of everyone else's. The usual waking hours begin at two or three in the morning, and then when the sunlight comes out, they go to sleep once again.

Withdrawal in the Household

This is something that is also frequently misunderstood, but people in withdrawal do not throw their weight around at home; instead, they tend to act shy around others. They are not necessarily cowardly when dealing with others, but tyrants with those close to them. If anything, the majority of them tend to avoid their family members even in the house, and it is not unusual to find people who barely set foot outside their own rooms. In our survey, we found that 60 percent of the respondents said that they either have no conversations whatsoever or their conversations are limited to only family members.

When withdrawal becomes particularly severe, people in withdrawal may coop themselves up in their rooms, refuse to take a bath, urinate and defecate in an empty can or jar instead of going to the toilet, or have other family members bring meals to their rooms. When this happens, they end up falling into a trap, whereby they have hardly any communication with others.

It goes without saying, but people in withdrawal hate for others from outside the immediate family—relatives and other people—to enter the house. They often become extremely upset even when workers come to do remodeling or similar work. When withdrawal reaches this extreme state, then hikikomori patients often are unable to do anything for themselves, spending the entire day in an absent-minded state, wrapped in a blanket, and letting time go by pointlessly.

Regression

Regression is something slightly different from the symptoms that I have described so far. This is not a word that describes a symptom as much as an explanation of the mechanisms arising from a psychological state. Originally, this term refers to when a grown individual moves backward to a less mature state on the path of personal development, but here I use the term more generally to mean "reversion to childhood."

In our survey, we found that 44 percent of hikikomori cases had involved "instability with family members" with an alternating pattern of aggression, on the one hand, and dependence and regression on the other. Also, 36 percent of respondents had demonstrated "reliance on parents and infantile behavior," for at least a certain amount of time. It is safe to say that these patterns of behavior arise as a result of regression.

The state of withdrawal often seems to bring about regression. This is my personal hypothesis, but in a certain sense, this phenomenon arises because the hikikomori patients are, in a certain sense, "healthy." Whenever anyone is placed in a limited space and has to rely for an extended period of time on others, there will be a degree of regression. Perhaps the most straightforward example is of a person who has been hospitalized. Patients who have spent a fair amount of time in a hospital—even patients who have significant positions within society—tend to show infantile and selfish tendencies that can strike others as quite unexpected. That is a natural reaction. It would be more of a problem if someone did *not* show any sign of regression whatsoever.

Anyway, let me return to the main point. People who have been in a withdrawn state for a long period of time often regress or, in other words, become increasingly childlike. As a result, they might do things like cling to their mothers, speak in wheedling, infantile voices, or express the desire to touch their mother's bodies. It is not unusual to find people in withdrawal who sleep in the same bed as their mothers or who cannot go to sleep without at least being in the same room. Waking up one's mother in the middle of the night and wanting to talk on and on for a long period of time can be seen as another sign of regression. There are even times when if the patients' desires are not fulfilled, then they will become fussy like a child, pestering their mothers in a tearful voice or kicking their mothers' legs and struggling with their arms.

The reason regression is such a problem is that it is often linked with violent fits. The majority of cases of violent behavior are a product of regression. I am not just talking about violence directed from a child toward his or her parents. Violence directed from a husband toward his wife is also the product of regression. It is easy to tell whether violence arises as a result of regression. One should just look to see whether the person is also violent toward people outside the family as well. If a person is polite outside the family but behaves like an angry despot in the house, then it is safe to say the behavior arises out of regression. Likewise, if a person is *always* violent, it seems safe to see that person as not having yet fully matured.

Violent Outbursts at Home

Here I must say a few more words about the subject of violent outbursts at home. Withdrawal and violent outbursts in the home are extremely closely related.

First, let me share some of the results of the survey. In the question about whether the respondents had shown a "combative attitude toward their family," we found that, if we include those who had demonstrated a combative attitude at least temporarily, 62 percent of the respondents had shown combativeness (which did not necessarily involve outright violence). Fifty-one percent of the respondents had demonstrated bouts of what we might term "violent outbursts at home," although in some cases, these bouts were just temporary. These results were compiled from different questions, and a large number of people fall into both the "combative" and the "violent at home" categories, but still, the finding that over half of the case studies we dealt with involved violent outbursts at home is surprisingly high.

As I stated before, violent outbursts arise out of regression. Strictly speaking, however, such outbursts are not the same thing as regression. If regression is taking a step down on the ladder of development and returning to a less mature state, a large number of people regress to become "good children" and do not go through a rebellious stage. What I am trying say is that violent outbursts at home do not necessarily come about simply because a person returns to a less mature state. Instead, violent outbursts are another symptom that one finds among certain people in regression.

There are various different types of domestic violence; however, all of them have the same fundamental roots. Let me jot down a list of the various types of violent outbursts that I have encountered.

- Striking walls, stomping on the floor

- Screaming in a loud voice

- Breaking glass windows; punching holes in walls; breaking dishes, containers, and other objects

- Dousing the house in kerosene and threatening to "burn the place down"

- Forcing one's siblings to play games, then rejecting them and hitting them

- Hitting one's mother out of revenge while listing all sorts of past grievances against her

- Hitting one's father as he steps in to stop violence against the mother

These kinds of violent outbursts are fundamentally wrapped up in a grudge against the parents. It is relatively rare that there are concrete reasons for the grudge, but one particularly common complaint is "It's my parents' fault I ended up like this." It is relatively easy to understand complaints such as "They used corporeal punishment against me when I was little," "They ignored me," or "They didn't understand me when I was going through a tough time," but sometimes individuals in withdrawal will voice complaints that sound like trumped-up charges. For example, they might say, "They made a nasty face when I asked them to do something for me," "They dozed off when I was trying to tell them something," or "When I asked them, 'You think it looks bad to have a son like me?' they didn't jump in and deny it." I believe it is important not to get into whether the person's claims—the claims that give rise to the violent tendencies—are grounded in reality. What is important is to know what the individuals are trying so hard to tell the family that they feel like they have to resort to violence to be heard.

Violent outbursts at home are closely related to a variety of psychological symptoms. One that is especially closely related to it is obsessive-compulsive disorder. As I mentioned briefly before, one often sees that when patients are trying to get the family involved in their obsessions, there can be severe outbursts when the family refuses to do what they are told or they fail to do it to the standards demanded of them. Later in this book, I say more about violent outbursts and how families can work to alleviate them.

Thoughts of Persecution

Some people who have been shut away from the world for a long period of time will say such things as "The neighbors are spreading rumors about me," "I was able to hear someone outside the house saying things about me," or "When the kids were walking by the front of the house, they were saying nasty things about me." These are called thoughts of persecution. Among psychologists, this symptom leads us to wonder if the person is perhaps experiencing auditory hallucinations or delusions. In situations where it seems highly probable that the things are not necessarily happening, we might say that the person is suffering delusions of persecution, but in reality, it is often difficult to determine whether or not they are delusions. If we include the respondents who reported mild thoughts of persecution, our survey found that 20 percent had experienced some form of "hallucinations or delusions."

I say more about this later, but if patients in withdrawal are experiencing these things, it is imperative to determine right away whether these are signs of schizophrenia. If the condition is not caused by schizophrenia, then these would be called "delusional thoughts," which makes them slightly different than outright "delusions." In the section about schizophrenia, I explain a bit more about the distinction between delusions and delusional thoughts.

Feelings of Depression

Emotional instability, especially feelings of depression, is a relatively common symptom among people in withdrawal. According to the survey, 31 percent of the respondents reported experiencing chronic changes in their emotional state. The percentage of respondents experiencing depression was 59 percent, if one includes mild cases. This is not the same as depression, but 53 percent of the respondents stated that they had experienced "feelings of despair, wanting to die, and feelings of guilt," if one is to include mild cases.

What is clear is that it is extremely easy to develop feelings of depression when in a state of withdrawal. It seems that cases of depression in the classic sense are rather infrequent. I say more about this in just a moment, but cases of withdrawal caused by the kind of depression we would identify as a psychological illness are relatively exceptional. Still, one does sometimes see withdrawal prompted by "emotional blocks caused by environmental factors" in mild cases of manic depression.

Are the despair and suicidal thoughts experienced by the people in our case studies completely unrelated to depression? I cannot conclude this definitively, but it is possible to react to these feelings by understanding and sympathizing with the withdrawn patient. The survey found that 88 percent of the respondents had experienced feelings of "isolation, boredom, and emptiness." I have already emphasized this several times, but it is clearly a mistake to see young people who have withdrawn from society as living peaceful lives of indolence. In reality, they are spending their days assaulted by feelings of impatience and despair over their inability to participate in the society beyond their immediate family. The fact that they do not have any real standing in society causes them to feel this way. For this reason, one could say that the fact that many of them are assaulted by feelings of despair and thoughts of suicide shows that their power of judgment is still intact. The major difference between their situation and clinical "depression" is that the patient suffering from clinical depression frequently thinks, "It's all too late, there's no turning back now." Many hikikomori patients, however, still are undergoing internal conflict, thinking they would like "to do whatever it takes to make a new start," and "the sooner, the better." However, because they do not feel that they have much time or space to carry this out, these thoughts do not transfer into hope, and unfortunately for them, these feelings just transform into irritation and despair.

Wanting to Die and Suicidal Thoughts

As I have stated before, people in withdrawal often spend their days assaulted by strong feelings of hopeless and emptiness. It is not unusual for them to consider suicide when these feelings become unbearable. Forty-six percent said that they had "wanted to die or planned suicide," and 14 percent had actually hurt themselves or had made failed attempts at suicide.

This number is certainly one to raise alarm, but on the other hand, it is perhaps still less than one might expect. This is not an especially high number compared with some other psychological afflictions. In my own experience as a psychiatrist, I have never had a hikikomori patient commit suicide who was not suffering from other psychological problems. One could draw various inferences from this, but I believe this attests to a healthy desire on the part of most to keep on living.

Other Symptoms

"Overeating" and "refusal to eat" are two other conditions that one might see manifest themselves temporarily among hikikomori. Such eating disorders are overwhelmingly more common among women, and in this case alone, I think it is necessary to consider treating the eating disorder first. When I have seen eating disorders among men, it seems these disorders manifested themselves only after an extended period of withdrawal.

Conditions that have the root cause in the mind but manifest in the body are called "psychosomatic." The most representative examples of psychosomatic illnesses are gastritis and high blood pressure, both of which arise as the result of stress, but eating disorders can also be psychosomatic. Of these psychosomatic conditions, the most common are ones that affect the autonomic nervous system. We saw such conditions in 66 percent of our patients. As I mentioned in the section about the reversal of night and day, irregular patterns seem to be the largest cause. No doubt, stress is also another major contributing factor.

Another symptom one finds among withdrawn patients is an obsessive concern about their own health. They might become obsessed with the questions "Am I sick?" or "Am I going to become sick?" even when they are not manifesting any illness at all. Sixty percent of our respondents reported some sort of "mental symptoms," including hypersensitivity to their own health.

One additional symptom is an addiction to intoxicants, including paint thinner and cough suppressants. (Of the issues that I have mentioned, this issue is perhaps the one that is most closely linked to misconduct.) Eighteen percent of respondents had at least one experience with intoxicants, and 6 percent of the respondents had experienced a chronic addiction.

Other Background Factors

Here I would like to talk about various factors, other than symptoms, that affect patients in withdrawal.

First, let me say a few words about the family structures of the people who served as our case studies. Most families had a father who had graduated from university and was at work, most frequently in some sort of managerial position, and a mother who had a high school education or higher but worked at home as a homemaker. Most of the families came from those who would be considered in contemporary Japan to be middle class or above. Nearly 70 percent of the families had no major problems in their domestic makeup, such as divorce or a father who was forced to live away from the family because of work. Based on my own experience counseling hikikomori patients, there seemed to be few patients who had what would typically be considered "big" problems, such as a broken family environment or abuse. If anything, withdrawal seems to appear in the most average Japanese families. This fact, in many ways, seems to support the idea that the problem is deeply linked to some pathology in contemporary Japanese society. I have the vague sense that probably this is something that we cannot fully account for with an unsophisticated problematic, such as the "increasing lack of energy among our youth." I suspect the problem is more complicated than that.

What about the numbers of children in the families? Eighty-five percent of the respondents came from a family with more than two children, including the patient himself or herself, and 60 percent were the eldest child—well over half. Of the total percentage, 49 percent of the respondents were the first-born son as well as the oldest child overall. Of course, not all first-born sons were the oldest child in the family, so if one were to look at just the ratio of the withdrawn patients who were first sons, the number is over half of all respondents. As a result, we can see that my earlier statements that men are more likely to experience withdrawal and the percentage of eldest sons is especially high are not ungrounded. These results are especially interesting, considering that in Japanese culture, many families place great expectations on the shoulders of the first son born into the family.

In response to the question about what the trigger was to send them into a state of social withdrawal, the highest number of respondents stated the reason was "unclear" (39 percent of respondents). The next highest responses were "problems related to people other than family" (38 percent), "discouraging experiences having to do with academics" (18 percent), and "changes in the school environment" (10 percent).

In response to the question about the first symptom of withdrawal, 39 percent responded "nonattendance at school," 29 percent responded shutting themselves in, and 25 percent responded apathy and listlessness. As for the period of withdrawal, the average length of time that passed between the beginning of the respondents' withdrawal and their first clinical treatment was 23 months, whereas the average length of time from the beginning of their withdrawal to the time of the survey was 39 months. Among our respondents, the longest period of withdrawal was 168 months (14 years) from the time of the first withdrawal until the time of the survey.

When we asked respondents when their symptoms first appeared, the most common response was the "first year of high school" at 23 percent, while the next most common response was "the second year of middle school."[4] In response to the question about when they were in the school system at the time of their first treatment at a hospital or clinic, 45 percent—nearly half—of the respondents said they had "no affiliation" with school at that point. The next most common responses were "first year of high school" and "second year of high school" in that order. These results reflect the fact that it is often a matter of years between the time that people first start having problems and the time that they come for counseling. When we asked about educational background, the most common answer was "graduated from middle school" with 31 percent, then "graduated from high school" at 29 percent, and "dropped out of high school" at 18 percent. In regard to their current work status, 48 percent stated that they were "unemployed," and 44 percent responded they were "students."

In response to our question about the trigger for the "first symptom" of the "social withdrawal," the majority of respondents said that it had to do with "relations at school." The average age for the first symptoms were 15.5 years old, so most were students at the time, and the answer "relations at school" makes a great deal of sense. "Nonattendance at school" showed up as the first "symptom" among nearly 70 percent of the respondents, and if we are to add to that the number of people who also started not attending school at some point along the way, the number of people in withdrawal who experienced some period of not going to school was nearly 90 percent. This is clearly an important sign.

Not attending school can be an extremely important sign that adolescents and early adults are failing to adjust to their surroundings. In some cases, it can also be an extremely important sign of the beginning of some sort of psychological ailment. The results of our survey back this up. As I mentioned earlier on, a number of surveys have tried to assess the number of students not going to school in Japan, but there have not yet been enough surveys that track the future development of such students. I believe that our survey will be helpful in understanding the development of certain groups of students who stop attending school. In any case, a certain proportion of students who stop going to school go down a path of social withdrawal, and as their period of isolation grows longer, the more difficult it is for them to recover. These are not facts we should treat lightly.

What Is the Psychological Reason for Withdrawal?

If withdrawal is a problem that arises from a psychological reason, then what is that reason? Certainly, the immediate triggers often come from setbacks at school—things like a broken heart, bad grades, failure at exams, bullying, and so on—but are those the only reasons? If those do provide the reasons for the ailment, why would those external experiences produce such long-lasting effects? Of course, patients suffering from certain types of psychogenic disorders do sometimes experience symptoms that continue long after the event that caused the disturbance is over. In many of those cases, however, the patients are not fully aware of the connection between the experience and the symptoms. A common pattern seen in many psychological afflictions is that memories of a difficult experience are locked away in the depths of memory but make themselves felt through the unconscious mind, thus causing symptoms to arise. In contrast to this, the patients in our case study could clearly remember the experiences that served as the trigger for their own withdrawal.

As I have suggested before, I am of the belief that the withdrawn state is often far more serious than the experience that provokes it. This is probably because "withdrawal" is not a condition that is caused by a single psychological factor. We can think of it as a system—a vicious circle, in which various psychological factors work together, and one external trauma gives rise to another. Indeed, it is entirely possible that it may have all started off with a drop in grades, conflict with friends, or being bullied; however, when individuals withdraw from the world and shut themselves up, they lose the opportunities for healing that interactions with other people can provide. Sure enough, other people do provide stress and can be a source of trauma, but if one gets rid of the help that others can provide, it becomes just about impossible to recuperate. It seems that one reason people in withdrawal have difficulty recuperating on their own is that they do not have any meaningful contact with others. What I am trying to say is the very fact of being in a state of withdrawal is itself traumatic in its effects. This is the only way to explain the psychogenesis of withdrawal and the unbalance that results from it. I explain this point in somewhat greater detail in a later chapter on the hikikomori system.

3 | PSYCHOLOGICAL AILMENTS
ACCOMPANYING WITHDRAWAL

The Importance of Early Diagnosis

As I explained earlier in this book, "social withdrawal" is not the name of a disease. Currently we do not have a single pathology that can appropriately describe the condition. There are people who believe that we should not use the terms *withdrawal* or *hikikomori* to describe a single ailment. In its own way, that argument makes sense.

Of course, there are several ailments other than the "social withdrawal" I am describing in this book that produce similar conditions. When the clinician first begins to treat a patient, he or she is busy trying to figure out what exactly is going on with the patient, so for the sake of clarity, I should probably briefly describe several other similar-looking ailments.

Before launching into an explanation of the ailments themselves, I would like to mention a few basic principles of psychology for the benefit of nonspecialist readers. First, there are the classifications of psychological disorders. One can divide up psychological illnesses into three categories based on their cause: psychogenic disorders, endogenous disorders, and exogenous disorders.

Psychogenic disorders are caused by different types of problems within the mind. These include diseases that arise as the result of shock, stress, or psychological wounds incurred during childhood. As a result, there is no visible abnormality in the functions of the brain, and one cannot diagnose the condition based on physical examinations alone. Neurosis, hysteria, and personality disorders are examples of psychogenic disorders.

Endogenous disorders are attributed to abnormalities, most likely in the functions of the brain; however, those abnormal functions are, in the end, not typically found through physical examination. Schizophrenia and manic-depressive psychosis are examples of endogenous disorders. (Schizophrenia is also sometimes called "split personality disorder." The name "split personality disorder" easily leads to misunderstanding and prejudice, so there have been a good number of people in recent years both inside and outside the field of medicine who have argued that the name should be changed. For instance, Dr. Kin Yoshiharu at the National Center of Neurology and Psychiatry has argued for the importance of referring to the disease as "schizophrenia." I also support this, so I have chosen to use the term *schizophrenia* throughout this book in the places where others might have used *split personality disorder* or other related terms.)

Exogenous ailments are also known as "organic diseases." In such cases, there is a material abnormality in the cranial portion of the nervous system, and this causes a disturbance in the functions of the brain, which then gives rise to the ailment. It is possible to diagnose these ailments through CAT scans, MRIs, and electroencephalograms. Epilepsy, mental retardation, and autism are all diseases believed to have exogenous causes.

If one were to think about the *social withdrawal* I defined in the last chapter in terms of the categories above, it would fall under the category of psychogenic disorders. Withdrawal also appears in conjunction with other psychological disturbances. For that reason, it is necessary to properly diagnose the patient and determine an appropriate course of therapy before starting to treat the disorder. The reason that so many clinics say "We can't treat the patient just through talking to parents alone; we need to speak to the patient himself or herself" is because it is impossible to properly diagnose people without meeting them directly. It only makes sense that we cannot start on a full-fledged course of treatment without a proper diagnosis first.

Probably the most salient issue in the initial stages of consultation with a patient in withdrawal is determining whether the patient is suffering from schizophrenia. If the patient has withdrawn because of schizophrenia, then the main part of treatment will involve taking medicine to alleviate the condition. In that situation, it is not unusual for a person to make rapid improvement simply through receiving the appropriate prescription. On the other hand, if patients are left to their own devices, then the condition can become chronic and sometimes result in complete changes in the personality.

So what kinds of diseases might send an individual into a withdrawn state? I comment on some of those conditions below.

Schizophrenia

First, how is one to distinguish between schizophrenia, the most serious of these ailments, and social withdrawal? Of course, a certain number of schizophrenic patients do withdraw from the outside world. Often, schizophrenics suffer from hallucinations and delusions, which show up clearly in abnormal speech and actions. In cases where signs of abnormality (what we would call "positive symptoms") are visible to everyone, it is relatively easy to diagnose the patient.

Another type of schizophrenia, however, has symptoms that are not terribly obvious. In cases when the patient has a rather light case (and sometimes even in cases he or she does not), it can be rather difficult to diagnose a patient as schizophrenic. In cases where the symptoms are not especially prominent, what is most obvious to the people around them is the patient's withdrawn state and apathy. We would call these "passive symptoms," in contrast to the positive symptoms I mentioned before. In these cases, it can be extremely difficult to determine whether the psychogenic reason is social withdrawal or schizophrenia.

Earlier, I mentioned the *DSM-IV* is the diagnostic manual used by psychiatrists almost everywhere in the world. Unfortunately, the *DSM-IV* is not very helpful in distinguishing between schizophrenia and psychogenic withdrawal. This is because one often sees conditions like the ones described as characteristics of schizophrenia—"restrictions in the range and intensity of emotional expression," "social isolation," "failure to achieve what would have been expected for the individual," "dysfunction in one of more major areas of functioning," clear difficulty in "maintaining hygiene," reduced "fluency and production of thought and speech," "inability to initiate and persist in goal-directed activities"—in patients in social withdrawal as I defined it in the previous chapter.

So if a person does have clear hallucinations and delusions, is it safe to diagnose him or her with schizophrenia? Actually, it is not quite that simple. The reason is that, as I mentioned in the previous chapter, there are hikikomori patients who experience delusional behavior as a result of their state of withdrawal. It is not at all unusual to hear people say things such as "the neighbors were talking about me outside the window" or "someone stopped their car in front of the house and was spying on me."

These complaints are extremely difficult to distinguish from the kinds of delusions that come from schizophrenia. Specialists too have been known make to mistakes—myself included. What I am trying to say is that it is not possible to make a theoretical distinction between "delusions" and "delusional thoughts." If I did try to force the issue and make some arbitrary distinction, then readers might start coming to conclusions that seem reasonable but really are not very helpful at all—conclusions such as "well, these delusions don't seem schizophrenic, so this might not be a case of schizophrenia." Nonetheless, I relay some of my impressions of the ways that schizophrenia and social withdrawal differ. Please bear in mind that I am not trying to make a firm theoretical distinction between the two.

First, the "delusional thoughts" of hikikomori patients are—at least to a certain extent—understandable if we try to think through the chain of cause and effect that led them to their current mind-set. We might recognize their thoughts as delusional, but it is still possible to sympathize with their feelings and understand the ways in which they feel they have suffered as victims. I say more about this later, but if we understand their feelings of inferiority and embarrassment, one can feel a certain degree of sympathy with them. I am making a sweeping generalization here, but it often seems to me that it is difficult to put oneself in the same shoes as someone suffering from schizophrenia.

In schizophrenia there is a sort of "strangeness" about the patient. It is often extremely difficult to put this strangeness into words. There is often a sense that something is not quite right—a feeling that is not necessarily completely conveyed when we simply call someone "bizarre" or "weird."

Let me give some relatively common examples of things that might happen with schizophrenic patients. Schizophrenics have been known to say things like "They were showing me on TV," then stop watching TV altogether, or they might complain that they are suffering because of "electrical waves or electromagnetic radiation" being sent out at them. There are also cases in which people mumble to themselves when alone or frequently burst into laughter, even though there is no one with them. One patient took a burning sheet of paper and threw it into the house of his next-door neighbor. Of course, I do not say that this kind of behavior is a definitive clue, but in cases where a patient does exhibit this kind of speech or behavior, I consider the possibility that he or she might be suffering from schizophrenia first.

In my opinion, the greatest difference between hikikomori patients and schizophrenics has to do with whether it is possible to establish enough communication with them. In the cases of social withdrawal, no matter how quiet a person might be, it is usually possible to use facial expressions or behavior to figure out more or less what he or she wants to say or is quietly complaining about. Through a certain amount of effort, the people around these individuals are usually able to understand their suffering. If one just gets used to their behavior, it should be possible to guess at what the problem is, even if the only thing the patients are doing is stamping their feet on the floor and not saying a word.

In cases of schizophrenia, however, this is difficult to do. It is often difficult to figure out why the person is doing what he or she is doing. If the person is behaving in ways that are not logical or that involve sudden, repetitive bursts of strange behavior, one should probably consider schizophrenia first.

I learned an interesting technique to distinguish psychogenic withdrawal from schizophrenia from the psychiatrist Dr. Kasugai Takehiko. He suggests having the therapist write a letter or a memo, and then sending it to the family to give to the patient. If the patient takes it in hand and reads it, then the illness is likely psychogenic withdrawal, but if he or she shows no interest in it whatsoever, then one should suspect that the patient is suffering from schizophrenia. Based on my own clinical experience, this has proved an extremely helpful technique.

In most cases of social withdrawal, it may seem that hikikomori patients are avoiding the rest of the world, but in reality, they have an earnest desire for contact with other people. In most cases of schizophrenia, however, the patient is trying to completely avoid all contact with others or has no interest in them whatsoever. These guidelines for differentiation may not be 100 percent accurate, but I still believe that they can be quite helpful in clinical situations.

Student Apathy and Retreat Neurosis

"Student apathy" is one of the most important factors in nonattendance at school, which as I mentioned previously is one of the most obvious problematic behaviors associated with withdrawal. Student apathy is a troubling issue that has gained a great deal of attention since the 1970s. To put it briefly, it refers to the failure of college students to attend school; however, because there are a number of differences between people who suffer from this and regular people who simply skip class, research has treated it as its own distinct concept.

First, let me say a few words about student apathy. When Paul A. Walters first talked about this subject in 1961, he described student apathy as the tendency, especially common among male students, to avoid competitive situations, such as test taking. As a result, it becomes difficult for such people to develop their identities as men, and they fall into a continuing state of apathy. This "avoidance of competition" is also said to involve a sort of aggressiveness.

Kasahara Yomishi, a professor emeritus of psychiatry from Nagoya University, worked to introduce this concept into Japan during the 1970s and 1980s, thus laying the foundations for research that surpassed that conducted in the United States, where the term was first born.

Kasahara did not just limit the pathology of student apathy only to students; he put forward a new clinical concept of retreat neurosis (taikyaku shinkei shō). I have listed its main characteristics below.

- It afflicts primarily college-aged students, especially men.

- Patients express lack of interest, apathy, lack of emotional affect, loss of goals, loss of direction, loss of a reason to live, or uncertainty about their identities.

- Because they do not suffer anxiety, irritation, depression, anguish, regret, or other painful emotions, they often do not actively seek out treatment on their own.

- They feel no severe discord in their current situations, so they do not make any effort whatsoever to extricate themselves from it.

- They are not unaware that there is something wrong with them. They are sensitive to relations with others, and they can be severely hurt when someone scolds them or rejects them. They have a tendency to avoid all situations except those in which they know they will certainly be accepted.

- Distressing experiences are not turned inward to create internal discord; instead, they are turned outward and manifested in behavior. In other words, distress is expressed through apathy, retreat, and other related behaviors, such as betrayal. It is rare to see it transformed into extreme behaviors such as violence or plans for suicide.

- Their indifference toward work and school is only partial; they often put a good deal of energy into part-time jobs or other work that is not their mainstay.

- They are very sensitive to whether or not they are superior or inferior to others, or whether they are winning or losing; as a result, they tend to avoid situations in which they think they might lose or suffer some form of contempt.

A number of these characteristics can also be found among young people in a state of withdrawal. Withdrawal among college students in particular tends to manifest characteristics similar to those of student apathy described above.

One does ordinarily find discord or even violent behavior with people in withdrawal. On this point, there seems to be some divergence from what is described in the research on student apathy, but when one thinks about the sources of the conflict, the differences are not all that pronounced.

Let me explain. The conflict experienced by people in withdrawal is, in most cases, caused by dissatisfaction with their current situation or feelings of inferiority. If they are still enrolled in university, then it is sometimes possible for them to compartmentalize those feelings of conflict for the time being. Most likely, they can do so because their social position as a college student gives them a strong sense of belonging somewhere. Also, society is quite tolerant of college students, since their position confers on them a certain social status. In the setting of the university, there are all sorts of people—it is not unusual to find exchange students from other countries or people who have failed their examinations and have to study for another year. It is also just about the only social sphere in Japan where society allows people to act moody and fretful, and then it does so largely because of their youth. One's years in school are relatively free of obligation and expectations about productivity, so it can be a relatively pressure-free environment in some ways.

Even if one is able to compartmentalize one's feelings of conflict while in college, however, it is not possible to do so after graduation. In my experience, it is not unusual for people who begin with student apathy to end up in a severe state of social withdrawal. It is not uncommon for people who do not attend university also to express their strong emotional conflict in ways typically associated with social withdrawal, if they have a great deal of trouble interacting with other people.

I believe that it does not make a great deal of sense to draw strong distinguishing lines between student apathy and social withdrawal. For that reason, in this book, I treat student apathy as one manifestation of social withdrawal.

Avoidant Personality Disorder

Doctors have been using this diagnosis in cases of social withdrawal increasingly often in recent years. Avoidant personality disorder is a psychogenic disorder. However, it is still questionable whether one can completely explain the situations of people who are in withdrawal—people whose symptoms are still in the process of manifesting—as manifesting a pervasive "personality disorder" (as avoidant personality disorder is defined).

According to the diagnostic criteria of the *DSM-IV*, avoidant personality disorder is described as having the following characteristics.

> A pervasive pattern of social inhibition, feelings of inadequacy, and hypersensitivity to negative evaluation, beginning by early adulthood and present in a variety of contexts, as indicated by four (or more) of the following:
>
> 1. avoids occupational activities that involve significant interpersonal contact, because of fears of criticism, disapproval, or rejection
>
> 2. is unwilling to get involved with people unless certain of being liked
>
> 3. shows restraint initiating intimate relationships because of the fear of being ashamed, ridiculed, or rejected due to severe low self-worth
>
> 4. is preoccupied with being criticized or rejected in social situations
>
> 5. is inhibited in new interpersonal situations because of feelings of inadequacy
>
> 6. views self as socially inept, personally unappealing, or inferior to others
>
> 7. is unusually reluctant to take personal risks or to engage in any new activities because they may prove embarrassing

Quite a few of these diagnostic criteria also apply to people in social withdrawal. Still, although there is much in common, in reality, these diagnostic criteria are used to describe people who have a strong tendency to feel fear of other people. I am not saying that it is a mistake to apply this diagnosis to adults who are in a state of social withdrawal. As I explain in the section "International Comparisons" in chapter 4, I think we should try to be more specific if we want to think of standardized ways to deal with the issue.

One reason that I personally have a difficult time accepting this diagnosis completely is that I do not put a lot of faith in diagnoses involving "personality disorders." The diagnostic standards used for avoidant personality disorder often describe stages that we frequently see people pass through during their adolescence. In such cases, I am reluctant to diagnose a person as having a "personality disorder." I suspect that it might be more effective and meaningful instead to think of them as having some sort of psychogenic disorder, broadly defined, and to figure out a proper course of treatment.

Borderline Personality Disorder

In recent years the media have started talking a lot more about "borderline personality disorder," mentioning "borderline cases" (*kyōkairei*) and using the Japanese transliteration of the English word *borderline* (*bōdārain*) with greater frequency. In a nutshell, borderline personality disorder refers to cases in which people's relations with others and emotions are extremely unstable, and they frequently act violently or make failed attempts at suicide. The term describes people whose attitudes toward things and others tend to be divided into two extremes—good and bad. Moreover, they often experience feelings of emptiness and a vague sense of rage, and they are not good at being alone, but they are also unable to build stable personal relationships. When put this way, it may seem as if there is very little relationship between them and people in a state of social withdrawal. Most importantly, one characteristic of borderline cases is that they make do without relating to other people. In this regard, they are the opposite extreme from a person in withdrawal.

Still, the distinction is not simple to make. I have often seen that as patients in a typical state of social withdrawal progress in their treatment, they gradually begin to develop borderline characteristics. It is especially common for this kind of change to occur when they are in the hospital undergoing treatment. It is difficult to determine beforehand exactly which sort of patients will undergo that sort of transformation, as one does not know until commencing treatment.

Why does this happen? Kasahara pointed out that there seems to be some overlap in the pathologies of people experiencing student apathy and borderline personality disorder. Among the pathologies identified as characteristic of borderline personality disorder are problems of personal identity, splitting, the inability to experience pleasure, and feelings of emptiness. These are all things frequently seen in cases of social withdrawal, too. Kasahara also noted that whereas one tends to see borderline patients transform their feelings into behavior—namely, violence and attempts at suicide—patients experiencing student apathy tend to transform their feelings into behavior "passively" by withdrawing from their lives in society.

Let me share a few of my own personal thoughts on borderline personality disorder. People whom we identify as borderline patients have the same tendencies that we all possess to a greater or lesser extent; they are just expressing them in an extreme form that might not necessarily be pathological. For instance, in our everyday lives, we employ the "projective identification" that is considered pathological in borderline cases. That is what is happening when we are angry at our friends, but at the same time, conversely, we can sense they are angry at us. The issue seems to be a matter of degree; psychological conditions considered ordinary among most people are manifested in extreme forms among patients with borderline personality disorder. There is no clear boundary that separates us from the borderline personality cases, just as there is no line that clearly delineates between "health" and "illness." Moreover, it is not especially unusual for a healthy adult to begin engaging in seemingly borderline behavior in certain kinds of relationships with others. People sometimes say, "Treatment is what creates borderline cases," meaning the question of whether or not one is seeing a psychiatrist is what really determines whether one has a "disorder." In a nutshell, it is entirely possible that people in a state of social withdrawal and who find themselves in positions that are far more pathological than those of normal, healthy people might sometimes begin to develop borderline tendencies.

Adolescent Delusional Disorders

Adolescent delusional disorder (shishunki mōsōshō) is a general term that covers a number of different kinds of delusions in which people experience thoughts having to do with the sorts of feelings associated with adolescence. Central to these are the fear of one's own gaze, the fear of having body odor (bromidrophobia), and so on. It does not matter how often outsiders tell the patient that these things are only in their imagination or that they are wrong; the impressions still do not change. In this sense, the thoughts are delusional, but there are a few things that make such thoughts different from those of a schizophrenic. First of all, the symptoms usually do not progress past a certain point. Second, apart from the strong beliefs visible as symptoms, the patients' daily speech and actions do not usually stand out as especially strange. Among the first to report on these kinds of cases were Uemoto Yukio, currently at Nagoya University, and his colleagues.

In a report published by Murakami Yasuhiko from Nagoya University, he reported that among people suffering adolescent delusional disorders, he found "a sense of being incomplete," a desire "to start over," and "thoughts of magical disconnection" (majutsu-teki tanraku shikō), such as the belief that one could go back in time and do things over. Also, there is a tendency for patients to rebel against the thoughts they believe others have of them. These characteristics also appear with social withdrawal. "Adolescent delusional disorder" seems to have much in common with social withdrawal.

Depression

As for the distinction between depression and student apathy, Kasahara has looked at several related diagnoses, including the "escapist-style depression" (tōhi-gata yokuutsu) described by Hirose Tetsuya at Teikyō University. Kasahara has listed the following characteristics of student apathy as being different from what one sees in depression.

1. There is no sense of despondency, grief, or guilt.

2. There are no autonomic nervous disorders, insomnia, or changes of mood within a single day.

3. It is possible for a patient to develop a depressive state as a secondary disorder, but those feelings are not central to the experience.

4. The patient does not seek help from others.

5. One does not see a lowering of activity across the full range of a person's life.

Also, according to Walters, the first person to write about student apathy, people experiencing student apathy "do not take all of the love that they can get from the outside world," like patients suffering from depression. If anything, people with student apathy are likely to reject others, feeling that the world does not include them. This appears to be a point of commonality with most cases of social withdrawal.

A number of points in the passage by Kasahara that I referred to above do apply to people in a state of social withdrawal, but there are others that do not apply, especially points 1 and 5. The kinds of "bodily symptoms" that one finds in point 2 and that are necessary for a diagnosis of depression—especially insomnia, loss of appetite, and a depressed emotional state in the morning—are not especially pronounced in cases of social withdrawal. Another major difference with depression is the sense that the "depressive state is not a primary condition," which we see mentioned in point 3. But perhaps the biggest difference of all is that if a patient is suffering from depression, it is possible to treat him or her with medicine. Thanks to progress in antidepressants, it has become possible to expect that nearly 100 percent of patients suffering from routine cases of depression can recover through a prescribed course of medicine. Of course, in the case of social withdrawal, medicine can be partly effective, but in most cases, one cannot really expect such dramatic results.

Schizoid Personality Disorder

This diagnosis corresponds more or less to the psychological illness of "schizothymia." This refers to people who tend, as a personality trait, to be introverted and fond of solitude, and thus tend to withdraw socially. These tendencies are also shared with some of the withdrawn patients we have seen. In comparing schizoid personality disorder to student apathy, Kasahara lists the following major differences.

1. (In student apathy) there is little of the deep suspicion of others, the tendency to isolation, the passivity toward things, or the "coldness" and "hardness" in attitude.

2. (In student apathy) the patient was often active before the problems began, and there is the possibility that through treatment, the patient will recover.

There are some other characteristics that the *DSM-IV* raises as signs of schizoid personality disorder but that differ from the signs seen in typical cases of social withdrawal. I have listed those below.

3. Appears indifferent to the praise or criticism of others.

4. Neither desires nor enjoys social relationships.

If anything, these two points show tendencies opposite to those in cases of social withdrawal. People in withdrawal want to be praised more than usual and tend to be excessively sensitive to criticism. In short, people in withdrawal typically harbor a strong desire for relationships with others.

Cyclothymia

Cyclothymia is a diagnosis that has been getting a great deal of attention in recent years. Put in very simplified terms, it is much like a mild case of manic-depression. This diagnosis is used mostly in America, but in Japan it is not used very often, and there have been almost no reported cases. Clinical observation, however, has noted patients who experience repeated cycles of heavy depression and hypomania. In America many researchers have been writing about this ailment, most notably Hagop S. Akiskal. It seems cyclothymia is often treated in the same way as a mild case of manic depression. If, however, it is allowed to develop for a long period of time, it frequently results in full-fledged cases of manic depression.

Cyclothymia tends to cause grave problems for the patient's social life when it develops early. Before the onset, patients have normal abilities and do not have difficulty in maintaining relationships, so it is sometimes the case that they pass through their student years without trouble. Once they go out into society, however, they often have a great deal of trouble maintaining a stable job, since they are prone to bouts of ups and downs and their behavior seems inconsistent. If they do get a job during one of their periods of hypomania, they repeatedly get into trouble or even get fired, lose their confidence, and fall into a state of depression. In terms of personality and behavior, patients with cyclothymia act quite differently than people in social withdrawal, but because of their behavior, certain people with cyclothymia end up going through a process of withdrawal similar to the kind of withdrawal that I described in the last chapter. The number of such cases is not enormous, but I personally have encountered five such cases, so it seems that such cases are not extremely rare either.

Patients with cyclothymia act quite differently than patients in social withdrawal, so it is not especially difficult to tell the two apart. Patients with cyclothymia are also more likely to improve with pharmaceutical treatment than people in social withdrawal. Nonetheless, if one makes a mistake in treating these patients, they sometimes become even more difficult to help than ordinary hikikomori patients, so one should not treat cyclothymia lightly.

4 | IS SOCIAL WITHDRAWAL A DISEASE?

How Psychiatrists Have Treated It until This Point

Is "social withdrawal" an illness? It is necessary to be clear on this point, and I try to answer this question more thoroughly in this chapter. If it is an illness, then it is necessary to discuss how to counter it, as well as how to develop a system of diagnoses and treatment.

Are there ways to minimize confusion if the number of cases increases to the point that specialists can no longer ignore the situation? I think that we should do our best to place social withdrawal squarely within the field of psychiatric medicine as it has existed until this point. Of course, when we consider cases that we encounter in psychiatry, we always project the assumptions of whichever era of medicine we belong to, and there are always things that do not fit adequately into our existing frameworks. But before we turn our attention to the new challenges that social withdrawal might pose, it is necessary to describe the situation as much as possible using what language we psychiatrists do have in common.

I have conducted a whole series of psychiatric investigations into the problem of withdrawal. In this chapter, I discuss the results of those investigations as well as how we should go about placing social withdrawal within the framework of psychiatry that currently exists.

Survey of Psychiatrists

From April to May 1992 I cooperated with Inamura Hiroshi of the Institute of Community Medicine at Tsukuba University to conduct a survey to gauge how psychiatry looks at social withdrawal. We contacted 303 people: 99 professors of psychiatry from university medical schools across the nation, 103 psychiatrists who are members of the Japanese Society for Child and Adolescent Psychiatry, and 101 psychiatrists who did not belong to the organizations listed above but did belong to treatment facilities throughout the nation.

We mailed out a questionnaire to all of the parties listed above and received 102 responses. In tallying the responses, we came up with some interesting results. Unfortunately, there was a great deal of discrepancy in return rates for each of the three groups of we targeted, and the return rate overall was not high enough for a proper study. As a result, our results do not have the authority of something one would find in a medical journal, but I would like to briefly introduce the results here for the reference of my readers.

In our survey, we asked respondents about any patients that they might have had who met all four of the following criteria.

1. Has been in a continuous state of social withdrawal for over one year.

2. Is most likely experiencing a disturbance that arose as the result of a psychogenic cause (in other words, that has an extremely low probability of being organic or endogenous in nature, perhaps because the doctor in charge ruled these out as possibilities).

3. Developed symptoms at some point before their late twenties.

4. Either has no other symptoms than withdrawal or only has symptoms that most likely arose as secondary symptoms (anthropophobia, obsessive-compulsion, domestic violence, a mild victim complex, etc.).

First, we inquired about whether the rates of such patients were increasing. Fifty-seven percent responded that they have "had experience with such cases, but do not feel that there is an increase in numbers," whereas 29 percent responded that they "feel that there is a recent increase in numbers."

In response to a question about what the respondents thought about the diagnostic tools currently available, 57 percent responded, "it is possible to diagnose them with the diagnostic classifications currently available, but those classifications are not necessarily precise enough," whereas 22 percent responded, "it is necessary to provide some sort of new diagnostic classification."

When we asked what the most proper diagnosis for such patients would be, 36 percent responded "avoidant personality disorder." Twenty-five percent answered that they "would make a diagnosis based on the accompanying symptoms," while 23 percent answered "retreat neurosis."

Personally, what surprised me the most about these results were two things: that the number of therapists who had *never* encountered such cases was relatively large and, conversely, that nearly one-third of the respondents thought that the number of such patients *was* on the rise. When it comes to dealing with such cases, the fact that nearly 79 percent felt that the diagnostic classifications as they have existed to this point are not precise enough or are incomplete seems to support my gut feeling. Most of the respondents chose multiple responses to the question about how they would diagnose such cases, leading me to believe that patients experiencing withdrawal are not currently being classified into a single diagnosis and that many therapists believe patients who are experiencing withdrawal could fall under several different kinds of profiles. Based on my own clinical experience, I can say that most hikikomori patients are diagnosed based on accompanying symptoms, leading to diagnoses of "anthropophobia," "obsessive-compulsive disorder," and so on. The reason is that psychiatrists see it as important to be able to communicate with other doctors and staff, so they choose diagnostic profiles that have already been established.

Opinions on the Necessity of Treatment

Let me continue with the results of the survey. In response to a query about the necessity of treatment, 50 percent responded that "treatment was necessary," whereas 48 percent answered that "treatment could be carried out on a case-by-case basis." In other words, virtually all respondents recognized the necessity of treatment in some form or another. When we asked about what sorts of cases would lead the patient to start treatment, we received many comments, including "treatment was desired by the patient or by the parents," "there was a suspicion of schizophrenia," and "there was a heightened fear that the patient may harm him/herself or others." The fact that almost all of the respondents suggested treatment was necessary is a fact of grave importance.

When we asked about what sorts of treatment respondents thought would be effective, 87 percent responded "psychiatric treatment," 67 percent responded "treatment with medicine," and 31 percent responded, "hospitalization or in-patient treatment within a psychiatric facility."

The response "psychiatric treatment" can be taken in a broad sense to refer to the various kinds of treatments that go on in the psychiatric world and that do not involve pharmaceuticals or physical stimulation. Although the words *psychiatric treatment* roll off the tongue in a single phrase, in reality, psychiatric treatment could involve a variety of different possibilities. In the survey we included an additional question asking what sorts of psychiatric treatments came to mind first: 54.2 percent responded "group counseling for the family," followed closely by 53.1 percent who responded, "person-centered therapy in an out-patient setting."

In Japan the practice of counseling the entire family within a group setting is not especially widespread, so we should interpret the fact that so many psychiatrists responded in this way as evidence that they see the families as being an important part of the equation. "Person-centered therapy," also known as the Rogers' method, involves first listening to what the patient has to say and having the therapist try not to be overbearing with giving directives. Perhaps this response reflects the fact that many people in withdrawal do not have a strong desire for treatment, and there is a tendency to drop out of treatment partway, so the therapist has little choice but to be receptive and relatively nondirective in his or her dealings with the patient.

If there is a fairly general consensus that the family are an important part of the picture, would it make sense to have just the family members come for consultations instead of the patient, especially considering that the patients themselves are usually not especially eager to come to the clinic? Sixty-four percent of the respondents said that they thought one could "expect some sort of improvement" if just the parents came, whereas 26 percent responded, "cannot say either way."

Opinions on the Prospects on Returning to Society

How should patients proceed after they have gone through treatment, been through outpatient treatment at a clinic, and are finally ready to return to society? We asked the doctors what sorts of activities they thought would be meaningful in helping patients return to society. The responses were as follows: "psychiatric day-care facilities" (56 percent), "a part-time job" (34 percent), "an acquaintance or relative's workplace" (33 percent), "an organization for people with similar hobbies" (25 percent); "a facility for people to 'hang out' where there would also be specialist staff" (22 percent), and "a workplace for people with psychiatric disorders" (22 percent).

In response to our questions about how patients would fare in recuperating from withdrawal, 63 percent said, "There is no typical course of recuperation"; 21 percent said, "It is possible they will have a good prognosis through receiving treatment," and 12.8 percent said, "The prognosis looks extremely grave, even with treatment." My thoughts about treatment more or less match the majority of the respondents. What I am trying to say is this. If we leave withdrawn people to their own devices and do not get them into treatment, their situation will develop in a variety of different ways, but if we succeed in getting them into treatment, then in many cases the prognosis for recovery and reintegration into society is good.

In the survey, I also received a large number of valuable comments in addition to the regular responses. Among them, there were doctors who made some very enlightening comments, pointing out that it is meaningful to prolong contact with the patient in providing treatment. The respondents mentioned the importance of "the point of contact with the therapist," "the sharing of space," and possible need to "have a mediator with the therapist."

In regard to helping the patient return to society, many of the respondents' comments suggested that the particular system of treatment could be determined only on a case-by-case basis. The respondents also frequently pointed out how difficult it is to put the patient on a proper path to recovery.

Those are the results of our survey. Overall, the responses seem to be unexpectedly close to my feelings about social withdrawal, and this gave me a great deal of courage with my own work.

International Comparisons

Is the problem of withdrawal something that belongs to Japan alone? This is a difficult question. The reason is that it is possible to answer both ways: yes it is, and no it is not. If someone were to ask, "In other countries, aren't there any examples of withdrawal like the ones you see in our country?" the answer would have to be, "Yes, there are." However, there are factors that are distinctive about the ways that Japanese culture treats a withdrawn person and handles the situation. Those factors are probably one reason that people in Japan who go into withdrawal tend to progress in certain, distinctive directions.

For quite some time now, I have been interested in how psychiatrists in other countries think about "withdrawal" as I have been describing it in this book. Fortunately, the spread of the Internet has made it increasingly possible to exchange e-mails with psychiatrists from various different countries. Almost immediately, I accessed the web pages of university psychiatric schools, psychiatric clinics, and organizations in several different countries and sent them e-mails. To my pleasure, I received a large number of responses. Their contents were quite interesting, so I share some of them here.

The American psychiatrist Paul Malloy believes that it is possible to treat withdrawal as a sort of phobia by a combination of antianxiety drugs and behavioral therapy. In regard to the difference between cultures, he believes there is a contrast between the individualistic society of America and the group-oriented society of Japan. Dr. Molly Blank, who is a specialist in clinical psychology, sees it as a type of anxiety disorder and says that people who start out by not attending school can end up in a prolonged, chronic state of social withdrawal even after becoming adults. She also states that when one compares cases that begin after adolescence with those that developed earlier in life, the cases that developed later follow a worse path. It is possible to treat patients with antianxiety drugs, and so on, but she believes one cannot hope that they will be able to make a full-fledged return to society. She says that withdrawal can be linked to "a fear of failure." It is only natural that there is an increasing number of individuals who, when confronted by an increasingly complicated world full of hard competition, try to retreat from it completely.

Dr. Isaac Marks, who works in England and has written about the subject of withdrawal, states that this sort of problem is not at all uncommon in England and understands it as a sort of general fear of society. Dr. Marks also comments that in the United States, withdrawal patients would probably be diagnosed as having avoidant personality disorder.

The Taiwanese psychiatrist Lawrence Lan, who has spent some time in the United States, also linked it with a phobia. He stated that he had not experienced too many cases in Taiwan, and he suggested there was a possibility that the issue of withdrawal was closely connected with social or cultural conditions. Another Taiwanese psychiatrist, Chao-Cheng Lin, also said that such cases were unusual in Taiwan. Dr. Lin says that there is a kind of person who stops attending school because of separation anxiety, but one should suspect that people in long-term withdrawal have either a social phobia, avoidant personality disorder, or cyclothymia.

The Thai psychologist Pramote Sukanich said that he had never encountered that sort of problem in Bangkok and threw back at me the entirely justifiable question, "What do people in withdrawal do about their living expenses?"

The French psychiatrist Denis Regua said that such cases do not exist in France and that withdrawal must be connected to Japanese culture and the Japanese lifestyle. Likewise, the psychiatrist René Casso suspected that this is a social phobia that occurs in the Japanese context. However, one anonymous French psychologist made the following worthwhile comment.

> In France, the situation is the same. One sees social withdrawal
> from around the time of the first year of middle school. Because
> many of them end up homeless, who knows how many cases
> there are? Usually they come from broken households that have

no paternal authority. One can only see it as a psychological disease. Where did they come from? They only depend on other people and do not act on their own. I have never seen any articles on them in France. We have only just arrived at the beginning of the problem.

When we put together these opinions, we see that the majority of the cases that I have been calling "social withdrawal" are classified either as "social phobia" or "avoidant personality disorder." If we set up the presupposition that this might be something else, then certainly we may probably begin to see new possibilities for treatment. Through these comparisons with different countries, I came to the conclusion that the problem of social withdrawal is a multifaceted issue that cannot be explained away as simply a problem of individual pathology. Certainly, if we were to take up individual cases, there is no reason we cannot treat them as "social phobia" or "avoidant personality disorder." Nonetheless, what makes this problem so different is that we are not able to completely account for it with those diagnoses *alone*. In that sense, the comment from the French psychologist is very important. In Europe, if people with this severe psychiatric problem do not get treatment and become adults, they will certainly end up on the streets. The notion that when the withdrawn person is in his or her twenties and thirties, his or her parents will continue to take care of him or her as long as possible—perhaps *that* is the part of the whole story, in other words, *that* kind of familial relationship and all of the conflict it continually produces, which is the part of the story that is uniquely Japanese.

5 | HIKIKOMORI SYSTEMS

Withdrawal Is Not Apathy

In this chapter, I would like to think about why social withdrawal happens and what its mechanisms are. Why do people "withdraw"? The reasons certainly are not simple. I myself am not sure I can answer the question adequately; however, I do think that it is worthwhile to try to move forward by inquiring into the issue and coming up with different hypotheses.

I would like to emphasize once again that what I have been calling "withdrawal" does not necessarily mean the same thing as apathy. It is true that people who are in social withdrawal might look "inactive" or "idle," but they are not "apathetic." I am sure of that.

I have done a fair amount of research on the mechanisms of apathy. In general, there are two general patterns having to do with illness and apathy. In the first, patients become apathetic as their illness develops into a chronic state. For instance, it is commonly believed that when schizophrenia or depression continues over a long period of time, the patient loses all sense of initiative; however, in working with patients who receive treatment early on, I have rarely seen the patients become apathetic and listless. One finds many cases of apathy and listlessness in patients who have been hospitalized for a long period of time in a psychiatric clinic. It is sometimes said that this apathy comes from living for a long period of time in an environment cut off from society or comes from the side effects of the pharmaceuticals being used to treat them. I think that there is a good possibility

that this is true. What I am trying to say is that apathy often seems
to be the by-product of human actions and that it is not necessarily
the outcome of the natural progression of illness. That being said, it
is also known that certain patients may fall into a state of apathy as a
result of mental retardation or brain trauma, and in recent years there
has been a good deal of attention paid to personality changes brought
about as the lingering results (or "sequelae," in medical terms) of external trauma to the head. It is possible that in cases such as those, a
patient might experience a pathological state of apathy.

The other state of apathy is what we might call "learned apathy."
This, of course, refers to a kind of apathy that is neither the result of
a mental illness nor a problem with the brain; instead, it arises as the
result of some psychological cause. Relatively early on, experimen-
tal psychology advanced a number of theories about the mechanisms
of apathy. For instance, the following experiment was conducted. A
dog that was kept in a cage was given random, repeated electrical
shocks without any warning. At first, the dog showed signs of being
upset, barking and writhing, but it gradually became increasingly
"apathetic," showing less and less of a reaction. In other words, even
though it was repeatedly receiving unpleasant stimuli, it learned that
it was unable to control them, and that was when the apathy set in.
Similar kinds of experiments with human beings have proved that we
also become apathetic in similar situations.

But does that explain the mechanisms of apathy one finds in
cases of social withdrawal? Actually, there is a book that explains
"withdrawal" and "apathy" from this point of view; however, I think
that that model is too oversimplified to be of much use. If anything,
I think that model explains only one of the many different types of
"apathy" that do exist. As human beings, we do not want to engage
in wasted effort; however, are we always acting with a purpose in
mind? The idea of "learned apathy" is not helpful in explaining cases
where people know that if they just put forth a little bit of effort they
can achieve good results, but they still loaf around and do not put
in the effort. We are contradictory creatures who will do things (or
not do things) that we know not to be in our best interests. People
in withdrawal are also like this. It is not the case that they do not do
anything because they think it will be a waste of time. If anything, it

is *because* they know that it is in their best interests to do something that they find themselves paralyzed. I do not feel that this kind of situation can be adequately explained by simply describing the patient as "apathetic."

Withdrawal Cannot Be Explained Simply as Individual Pathology

In the previous chapter, there was a discussion about student apathy. Many researchers have conducted investigations in that subject, including Kasahara Yomishi. Because some people in withdrawal fit that profile, I would like to say a few more words about that here. First, it is worth noting that the words *student apathy*, which we often use in Japanese transliteration *(suchūdento apashī)*, are sometimes literally translated into Japanese as *gakusei mukiryokushō* (lit. "student apathy-syndrome") using the same word *mukiryoku* ("apathy") I have been using throughout this section of the book. As I stated earlier, this affliction cannot be boiled down to simple apathy; instead, I treat it in general terms as meaning that the person does not show any desire for what their main task should be—in most cases, their schoolwork. I would like to add that Dr. Inamura Hiroshi did not use the word *withdrawal* to describe it, although he frequently used the transliteration of the English word *apathy (apashī)*.

Paul A. Walters, who made the first studies of student apathy, saw the causes as linked to a formative disorder in "masculine identification"—in other words, people see themselves as failing "to be masculine" and hate to fail, so they avoid competitive situations as a form of self-protection. Kasahara has also noticed that in addition, there are elements that seem to have much in common with borderline personality disorder, especially anhedonia (feelings of emptiness) and splitting (extreme opinions and attitudes toward other people and things).

If one thinks of "withdrawal" as a kind of "social phobia" or "avoidant personality disorder," then it might be possible to explain the behavior of certain patients a little more clearly. In other words, the former would explain withdrawal as a kind of fear, whereas the latter would explain it based on a pattern of behaviors that recurs over the course of the patient's life. Indeed, these explanations do apply to a certain portion of patients in withdrawal. If we look at the problem this way, it is possible to explain the pathology of certain withdrawal patients as having to do with external traumatic experience or as a problem in development.

These sorts of psychiatric explanations can be used in certain cases to understand the withdrawn state; however, that does not necessarily mean that it is possible to cure the withdrawn state through psychoanalysis. I say this because it is difficult to carry out psychoanalysis with socially withdrawn patients who do not necessarily want to be treated in the first place. Moreover, it is difficult to understand the whole problem if one views social withdrawal only as a question of individual pathology. The family and society are deeply implicated in the problem as well, so it only makes sense that psychoanalytic analysis, which as a fundamental rule takes the individual patient as its principal subject, will not be able to deal with the problem entirely on its own.

As long as one attempts to account for the problem of social withdrawal as grounded solely in the pathology of one individual patient, the way we understand it, as well as any therapeutic measures we take, will only be superficial. But there is an even more fundamental problem that precedes that. If we treat withdrawal as an individual problem, then we shut down any communication with the families of the patients, saying, "If the withdrawn person himself or herself doesn't come to see me, there's nothing I can do." Social withdrawal inevitably involves the family, too, even in those cases where a withdrawal arises as the result of an individual, psychological problem. The involvement of the family only makes the problem worse, and the pathology grows deeper. But that is not all. The social pathology at work in our country ends up reflected in it as well.

As I hinted in the section in the previous chapter about international comparisons, social withdrawal is not something that is seen only in Japan. Nonetheless, the cases of withdrawal we do see here in Japan proceed along a unique path. The peculiarities of that path reflect the cultural and social situation in our nation. For that reason, the problem of "social withdrawal" goes well beyond just being a problem of individual pathology; it should be given serious consideration in the fields of social psychiatry and public health. That way, the issue of withdrawal will not be examined only through psychiatric methods that treat the individual; it will take on a greater significance as scholars conduct casework and therapeutic interventions involving entire families. In this book, as I think about measures to cope with the situation, I also want to emphasize that is important to think about *how to carry out effective therapeutic interventions* rather than just how to treat the individual most affected.

Vicious Circles in Relationships with Others

As I mentioned before, the very act of withdrawing from society is itself traumatic. In other words, the longer the period of withdrawal and the more serious the isolation, the more likely it is that the patient will fall into a vicious circle that will only make the withdrawal worse. In ordinary diseases within the body, when individuals grow sick, their bodies will react naturally with various therapeutic measures, including immune responses, and if those work, individuals begin to recuperate from the sickness. In the case of withdrawal, however, the unhealthy state has the function of making the situation even worse and even prolonging it. Why is that?

The first reason has to do the fact that there are multiple causes for "social withdrawal." As Nakai Hisao, a professor emeritus from Kobe University, once noted, psychiatric ailments that arise because of simple psychological reasons typically get better by proceeding along a simple path of development. Conversely, ailments that proceed along long, complicated paths usually do not have a single cause; instead, they are caused by a combination of multiple different factors, and this often impedes attempts at treatment. For instance, it seems the reason the trauma of being bullied lasts for so long has to do with the fact that the bullying itself usually continued over a long period of time, and as a result the trauma developed in complicated ways. The chain of events that leads a person to withdraw from society is certainly not simple. I say more about this later, but I believe the emotional situation for many people in withdrawal is usually so knotty and confused that it is not even effective to think about cause and effect; however, because the situation is so knotty, the patient falls into a vicious circle, and that only makes the situation that much more unclear. I try to explain what I mean in a slightly easier way using schematics.

When one looks closely at the problem of social withdrawal, one sees it has to do with problems in relating to other people. I would like to try thinking about the multiple causes for withdrawal by dividing them into three arenas, based on who is involved. The three arenas are (1) the individual, (2) the family, and (3) society in general.

I suspect that with withdrawal, there is some kind of vicious circle going on in *each* of these three arenas, and that is the reason that the withdrawn state ends up prolonged over a long period of time. To a greater or lesser degree, these vicious circles can occur with almost all mental illnesses. What is so conspicuous about withdrawal, however, is that these three arenas have a tendency to affect each other negatively and shut one another down.

With other mental illnesses, it is often the case that even when people fall into a vicious circle at the individual level, the family works with them and helps them break free from the problem. Even when the family has unhealthy dynamics that make it hard to escape a vicious circle, it is sometimes possible for individuals to make contact with society and form interpersonal relationships that will help them solve the problem. It is not uncommon that through temporary hospitalization, the patient gets away from the family, undergoes treatment, and becomes better. It is often the case, however, that patients who have recovered from withdrawal during hospitalization go home and slip back into their old patterns of behavior. The reason simply has to do with the fact that the family fails to treat them in a way that encourages their mental well-being.

For people in a state of withdrawal, the routes between the "individual and family" and the "individual and society" are completely shut down. As a result, the only thread of hope lies in getting the family to cooperate. In reality, it is often the case that treatment that involves earning the understanding and cooperation of the family can allow the person to recover. In most cases, however, there is a vicious circle at work in the relationship with the family, and the situation just gets worse and worse.

Unfortunately, the more these vicious circles go wrong, the more likely they are to stabilize, almost as if they were functioning as a single, independent system. And once these begin to function as a stabilized system, then it becomes difficult to stop the cycles through small doses of treatment.

I call these vicious circles "hikikomori systems," and I believe the fundamental principle for any kind of treatment involves thinking about how to disengage those systems. Of course, the ideas that I am presenting are only one possible hypothesis, and I might be going too far by simplifying the reasons for withdrawal this much; nonetheless, I believe that thinking about withdrawal as a system is significant precisely *because* it is so simple and straightforward. At the very least, it becomes easier to explain the various different situations of people in withdrawal through this model, and I believe it will prove effective in helping us devise better plans for treatment.

The Three Systems of Individual, Family, and Society

In Figure 1, I have provided two diagrams of what I call a "healthy system" and a "hikikomori system." In a healthy system, all three systems have a point of contact and are working. By point of contact, I mean to say that there is an open and functioning channel of communication. The individual is communicating with his or her family in the course of everyday existence, and they continue their lives, each affecting one another. The individual also communicates with society in places such as the school and in the workplace, and through them, society affects him or her. Through their lives and activities in various arenas, the family also has an open route of communication with society, and the family and the surrounding society affect one another. Of course, this is an idealized model, and in real life, communication does not always go smoothly. In most cases, however, they do not lose their "point of contact" entirely—in other words, they do not find themselves in situations where all channels for communication are cut off completely.

In the hikikomori system, however, the points of contact have been cut off from one another and no longer function. Now some readers may find themselves thinking, "No, that can't be. The individual talks to his or her family frequently, and the family has plenty

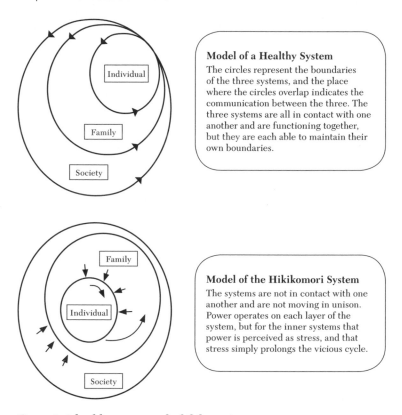

Model of a Healthy System
The circles represent the boundaries of the three systems, and the place where the circles overlap indicates the communication between the three. The three systems are all in contact with one another and are functioning together, but they are each able to maintain their own boundaries.

Model of the Hikikomori System
The systems are not in contact with one another and are not moving in unison. Power operates on each layer of the system, but for the inner systems that power is perceived as stress, and that stress simply prolongs the vicious cycle.

Figure 1. A healthy system and a hikikomori system.

of contact with the outside society through work, school, and so forth. Isn't what is missing the connection between the individual and the surrounding society?" The question that I would ask in return is this: does the "point of contact" involve real communication? If there were real communication between the individual and the family, then that would just make the situation all the more difficult.

For real communication to be possible, it cannot be a one-way street, where one of the two parties is just talking to the other. Reciprocation is an essential element of communication. Communication is not *real* communication if the individual does not listen to what his or her family has to say and just delivers an unbroken litany of his or her own complaints. It is surprisingly easy to overlook this point. The point is that "simple conversation" and "communication" are quite different things.

For the remainder of this chapter, I explain how the hikikomori system functions in each of the three arenas.

The Inability to Accept the Intervention of Others

Let's start with what the hikikomori system means for the individual.

As I have explained previously, the person who is in a state of social withdrawal typically feels a strong sense of conflict. As I have already shown, this conflict frequently leads to a variety of psychological symptoms. From those symptoms, it is possible to fall into a vicious circle. A fear of others, obsessive-compulsive disorder, and delusions of persecution all make it that much harder for the individual to participate in society. To make matters worse, the majority of these symptoms will not get better without participating in society or receiving some sort of treatment. The worst misfortune to befall people in withdrawal is that even though their symptoms are progressively getting worse, they find themselves in situations where they feel the need to withdraw even further.

Also, as I explained earlier, the very fact that a person is in a withdrawn state inflicts more psychological damage. Physically, the person might begin to stay up nights and sleep during the day, or he or she might develop insomnia, and those things just spur on the reversal even further. In this way, the withdrawn state is rather like an addiction. I say this because with addictions, there are various vicious circles that operate as a single system, and these just make the addiction that much worse. For instance, alcoholics often feel extremely guilty about their drinking. Still, even though they feel guilty—or to put it more precisely, *because* they feel so guilty—they end up drinking all the more and sink deeper into the quagmire. It is rather like the story of the drunkard in Antoine de Saint-Exupéry's book *The Little Prince*. The Little Prince asks the drunkard why he drinks, and he responds that he drinks because he is ashamed. When asked why he is so ashamed, he says that he is ashamed that he drinks. Pathological behaviors give rise to new conflict, and that merely strengthens the behaviors—it is this particular process that is a characteristic of addictive behavior. One sees a similar kind of vicious circle in the behavior of people in withdrawal. Individuals see their withdrawal as the "behavior of a loser," and this makes their feelings of self-hatred all the worse, leading to a deeper withdrawal—a vicious circle.

In ordinary circumstances, relationships with the family and other people are what stop the cycle from getting worse. These days, most people believe it is almost meaningless for an alcoholic to try to stop drinking on his own. Gregory Bateson has said that trying to do so is like trying to lift yourself up in the air by pulling on your own shoestrings. The most common treatment for addiction today is to enlist the help and guidance of the family while having the addict participate in a self-help group. In other words, it is important to have the family and other people participate in the process. If the source of the vicious circle is oneself, then it is absolutely necessary to let others intervene and proceed to treatment.

We can apply this little bit of common sense to the treatment of people in social withdrawal, too. The reason people cannot extract themselves from their state of withdrawal is that they hate this kind of intervention from other people more than anything. On the other hand, however, people who have steeled themselves and made up their mind that they are going to accept the help of others are able to return to society, almost without exception. I have observed this in working with patients, so I know that it is not possible to deal with withdrawal if we try to deal with it only from the standpoint of individual pathology.

What I am trying to say is this. Even though there might be several, different aspects involved in the individual sickness that started the whole process of withdrawal, as long as those reasons are psychogenic in nature, once people enter into an extended period of social withdrawal, they will end up continuing down that path and stay in a state of withdrawal that they cannot escape from on their own. As long as they are in that situation, the best plan of action is not to continue to be preoccupied with the beginning of the illness and keep trying to diagnose what went wrong early on. More important than trying to figure out what caused it is realizing the phenomenon of "social withdrawal" represents an entire system, and one must provide treatment and guidance with that in mind.

Lack of Communication

Next, let's look at the "family system" (see Figure 2). The family members who surround the person in withdrawal are also caught up in a vicious circle. First, the individual goes into withdrawal, and as the period of withdrawal grows longer, anxiety and irritation grow within the family. In their anxiety, the family gives the individual various kinds of stimulation, hoping to get him or her to change his or her behavior somehow. Frequently, this "stimulation" involves delivering speeches based on sound advice, or sometimes, it involves little more than yelling at the individual to get up and go. This stimulation, however, does nothing but add pressure and stress to the individual and does not help him or her become more active. If anything, the more stimulation he or she receives, the more likely he or she is to sink deeper into a withdrawn state. This then just makes the family that much more anxious and irritable, and they repeat the stimulation, although half-aware that it is not going to do any good.

As I have made clear already, the thing that causes these vicious circles to form is a "lack of communication." The one-way stimuli the family gives to the individual cannot be considered real communication precisely because it is so one-sided. The family's words do not reach the person in withdrawal at all. All that happens is that the family's anxiety, dissatisfaction, and irritation drive the individual into a corner.

In the behavior of withdrawn individuals, there is some sort of hidden message. That much is certain. If the family can grasp exactly what that message is at an early stage, that alone can sometimes be enough to help put the individual on the path to recovery. Even in cases when the individual has been in withdrawal for a long period of time, it is possible for the family to prevent the vicious circle from getting worse by sympathizing with the individual and understanding where he or she is coming from. Listening for messages, understanding while sympathizing—these things are what make deep, meaningful

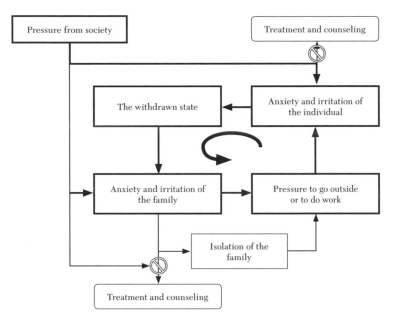

Figure 2. Vicious circles for the hikikomori.

communication possible for the first time within the family. It is only this kind of deep communication that has the ability to stop the vicious cycles in the family from getting worse.

The Disconnect between the Family System and the Social System

Then what about the "social system"? I mentioned earlier that in the hikikomori system, the three systems of individual, family, and society are all detached from one another. You might think to yourself, "But doesn't the family at least have some point of connection to society through the workplace or other institutions?"

I should probably clarify a bit further and say that when I emphasize that there is a disconnect between the three systems, I mean to say that they have lost a point of connection when it comes to the problem of the withdrawn person. Yes, even families who are extremely forward-thinking and participate actively in society tend to be close-lipped when it comes to talking about their own child being in a withdrawn state. Families worry about what people will think and try to hide it, or sometimes they try to figure out some way to solve the problem on their own without consulting with anyone. Psychologists have often found that in the course of individual development, the tendency to "keep to oneself" significantly slows a person's ability to solve adolescent problems. What I would like to emphasize here is that the disconnect between the family system and the surrounding social system is exactly the same sort of "keeping to oneself" that inhibits progress toward solving the problem. In a certain sense, it is no exaggeration to say that the family is also in a state of social withdrawal.

It is this tendency to keep to oneself that causes a disconnect between the "family system" and the "social system." Even though there is a separation between the two, it frequently happens that the family falls into a vicious cycle of its own. The family tries to stay independent and avoid the opinions of others, but at the same time, they lose the opportunity to seek out treatment or counseling because that would mean getting other people involved. That simply reinforces the tendency to keep to themselves. It seems to me that the tendency to "keep to oneself" on the part of the parents is characteristically Japanese. Instead of the "American-style" withdrawal in which everyone, including the family, avoids society altogether, the family continues to desire a connection with society—or perhaps it is because they want a connection all the more that they end up keeping to themselves. Because this setup prolongs conflict, it simply strengthens the hikikomori system.

That being said, how can we help the hikikomori system begin to function in a healthier manner? I explain that in detail in the next half of the book, which is dedicated to practical advice.

PART II.
HOW TO DEAL WITH
SOCIAL WITHDRAWAL

6 | OVERCOMING THE DESIRE TO REASON, PREACH, AND ARGUE

Recognizing "It Is Here"

It is extremely difficult to deal with people who are in a state of withdrawal. One reason is that our society has embraced a set of values that says, "If you don't work, you don't deserve to eat." As a result, we tend to take an overwhelmingly negative attitude toward social withdrawal; we deny that it is a problem with real roots and causes. In other words, there is a tendency to pretend that it is not there at all, even when it exists right before our very eyes. One result is a tendency to scold and yell at people in withdrawal, hoping to make them get up and go.

I have been dealing with patients in withdrawal for over a decade, but even so, I sometimes fall prey to the temptation to lecture or reason with my patients. There are often moments when the conventional complaints go through my mind—they are "spoiled" or "lazy," they are "griping about their rights but at the same time avoiding their responsibilities," or they are "shifting all their responsibilities onto their parents." All of these are just the sorts of things that you would expect people to say.

In dealing with people in social withdrawal, the first step is to struggle with these notions, which are so prevalent in our society. In other words, we must work to overcome our impulse to "deny" social withdrawal.

For that reason, it is important to recognize the truth that social withdrawal is here. In other words, one should not look at people in a state of withdrawal and think they have gone wrong somehow as a person. That is not the best way to deal with the issue. It is important to accept that the person in withdrawal needs some sort of help or protection. It is worth emphasizing once again that one is extremely likely to fail by "denying" the feelings and situation of the person in withdrawal—either through preaching, arguing, or getting violent with them.

The Limits of Effort and Encouragement

People who have been in a state of withdrawal for years and whose situations have grown chronic cannot recover without sufficient care from their family, as well as treatment by a specialist. This may seem a daring statement, but I am willing to assert this and to stand by my words. There are several reasons why I say this. First of all, I have never heard of a case in which a person in withdrawal improved without that kind of help. Second, among the hikikomori patients I have examined, there has never been a single case where someone has improved without participating in a regime of intensive treatment. But that is not all. Above all, I am extremely concerned when families try to handle a person in withdrawal all by themselves. It is precisely because I think it is a bad idea for the family to handle it themselves that I emphasize so strongly that people in a chronic hikikomori state do not get better through individual effort, scolding, and encouragement from the family. When one is dealing with long-term withdrawal, there are limits to the efforts that both the individual and the family can make, no matter how hard they try.

Of course, I am not saying that there is no possibility whatsoever that a person who is in the very earliest stages of withdrawing from society cannot recover through individual effort and external encouragement. Nonetheless, it goes without saying that there are a number of things that family members can do that are *not* helpful: using parental authority in a one-sided way to try to force the child to change, adopting an overly emotional attitude, refusing to listen to the child's opinions, and getting violent in order to make him or her obey. These techniques will only be traumatic to the person in withdrawal. Even if it looks like these techniques help get a person back "on the right track," they only delay a proper resolution to the problem, and it is only a matter of time before the person has a "relapse."

The Harmful Effects of One-Sided Passivity

When I say that making efforts and encouraging the patient are not effective, readers might wonder if that means that families should just sit back and be passive, taking whatever comes their way. That is going too far. It is obvious that one must adopt a fundamentally receptive stance for any treatment to be effective, but what people often forget is the commonsense notion that a framework is necessary for one to be receptive. People who try to be receptive to everything that the other party throws their way fall into the hands of the other person or become intoxicated with their own feeling of omnipotence, as if they were the greater party who is really in control. The question of how to establish the boundaries of one's receptivity is an extremely important theme in the clinical setting, too.

I believe that one-sided passivity is just as harmful as trying to reason with the patient in a one-sided way. The reason is that in both cases, there is not enough real communication taking place. The other party begins to behave in incomprehensible ways, thus causing confusion and consternation for everyone. When such situations arise, the first thing we try to do is engage in a dialogue with the person so that we may understand him or her and sympathize with what is going on. This is not so much behaving in a "clinical" fashion as simply acting on good, common sense. One should remember that it is not the case that every single person is necessarily simply waiting for understanding and a helping hand. Still, I cannot say that there are absolutely *no* cases whatsoever where a parent's impassioned attempts to reason with his or her child have helped the child move toward a greater participation in society. This kind of technique is not necessarily harmful in every single case; it does not necessarily damage the relationship of trust—provided, that is, that the parent does it well. The reason that I say that is because typically it is the person in withdrawal who wants more than anyone else to return to his or her rightful place in society.

If a child starts to avoid society and to go into a withdrawn state, the first thing the parents should do is to try asking the reason. Then the parents should make at least one thorough attempt to persuade the child that he or she can return to the world. It sometimes happens that through those attempts, the parents learn for the first time what kinds of troubles have been on their child's mind. Sharing opinions with one another on a relatively equal footing might sometimes lead to hard feelings, but even so, it still can often create the opportunity for good communication.

Traumatic Experiences and Recovery

I often draw a connection between the treatment of people in withdrawal and the process of maturation; however, the question "what does maturation mean?" is a difficult and thorny one. In the field of psychiatry, and especially in the subfield of psychoanalysis, "maturity" is an extremely important theme. For the purposes of this book, however, I provide a simple description of what maturity might look like from an extremely practical viewpoint. In my judgment, "a mature person" is the following: a person who has acquired a stable image of his or her own position as a social being and who is not overly damaged through encounters with other people. Of course that is only a working description, but as I treat my patients, I do so under the idealistic assumption that in most cases, patients want to end up in the situation I have just described.

How does "maturation" become possible? I believe it is through "acquiring immunity to trauma." The process of recovering from a psychological wound is not unlike the process of recovering from a communicable disease. What I mean is that in both cases, the person is left slightly changed in that he or she has something akin to an "immunity." It goes without saying that no one wants to catch a communicable disease, but if one does not have a certain level of exposure to germs and does not occasionally catch a mild case of some communicable sickness, then the immune system will not have any chance to develop resistance to bacteria and other germs. Two things are especially important here: first, the person has some experience with contracting a sickness, and second, the person is allowed to heal completely. One of the similarities between immunity and trauma is that they both come about through encounters with others. Of course, not every encounter with another person is traumatic, but isn't it true that encounters with other people important to you always inherently have the *possibility* of being traumatic? Perhaps the other has a violent disposition. Perhaps the other might represent some abstract principle, such as "death" or "loss." Or perhaps the other is someone you are attracted to but whom you fear might abandon you one day. How do we get over those sorts of prospects and learn to get by, accepting others as entities that we cannot control?

When people "mature," they undergo traumatic experiences, whether or not they like it. But that is not all that happens. It is also important that people who have experienced trauma are provided ample opportunity to recover from that trauma. They have the right to be allowed to do so. "Traumatic experiences and recovery" come as a set in the process of maturation. One cannot have maturation without these things. What makes this set of things possible is, of course, contact with others. When one gets hurt, it leaves one with an image of others that is traumatic and frightening; however, when one experiences healing through the support of others, that helps one acquire a more accurate image of others—it teaches that others are not always frightening. In that sense, acquiring immunity to trauma is a process of gaining an appropriate image of others.

The Withdrawn Person's Lack of Encounters with Others

In general, young people who are in a state of withdrawal are extremely frightened of being hurt. That is because they know all too well that even a single careless statement can make them feel as if their entire existence has been negated. Of course, we must show an appropriate amount of respect for those fears. However, it is also true that as long as they stay cooped up in withdrawal, they will not experience any psychological growth. No doubt the reason is already clear. In a life of withdrawal, individuals have no more contact with others, and therefore it is impossible for them to heal from the traumas they have experienced, even when those traumas are indeed real. To put it another way, the image they have of others is stuck—they perceive others as threatening beings that will simply bring about more pain.

Does that mean the family is not perceived as "other"? This is an excellent question, and if I were to venture an answer, I would say that they are not. In the eyes of people who have withdrawn from the world, their families are not "other." People in withdrawal seem to see their families almost as if they were a part of their own bodies.

The reason that they might engage in violent fits in the household is that they treat family members as if they were a part of their own selves and fail to recognize them as independent people. The reason I put so much emphasis on restoring channels of proper communication in the household is that it allows the family to be restored to their position as "others." Just as talking aloud to oneself is not real communication, the exchanges people have with family members whom they treat as part of their own selves are also quite far from real communication. When one is dealing with one's parents, it is only through recognizing that they are individuals with their own autonomous ability to act and make decisions that new pathways will open, allowing the possibility for real communication.

As I hinted before, it is difficult for people who are in a state of withdrawal and who have no contact with others to experience traumas that others would consider "real." Nonetheless, they are wounded, and they have been shattered by the belief "I have been terribly hurt." In the case of bullying, which involves a traumatic experience hidden from the view of others, it is essential to provide psychological support by giving the bullying victim a chance to recuperate and the full-fledged understanding of everyone around. One reason that the deep traumatic scars left by being bullied are still difficult to heal even after decades of recuperation has to do with the fact that the routes to proper healing are often sealed off. Recuperation for people who are in the early stages of withdrawal has to do with understanding the reasons *why* they are cooping themselves up while providing them ample opportunity to recuperate from their traumas. By doing so, it becomes possible in some cases for the person to get back on the right track through his or her own power.

When individuals have been in withdrawal for a long period of time, the situation is different. The longer the period of withdrawal, the more their own actions begin to harm them. That is the reason that one should not simply leave withdrawn individuals completely on their own. To extract them from the vicious cycle of self-destructive behavior (in other words, the hikikomori system I spoke about earlier), it is essential that others intervene. The essential question in treating people who have been in an extended period of withdrawal is how the intervention can be carried out most effectively.

Why Is Treatment Necessary?

Should all people in social withdrawal be treated, regardless of whether they want to be or not? Let me jump right to my conclusion. I think that yes, people in withdrawal should be treated. I do not, however, think that treatment should be carried out through coercion. We all know stories of people being held by force in psychiatric institutions—such forceful methods are *not* the best way to treat a patient in withdrawal. At the same time, even in situations where the person has refused treatment, the parents *do* have the right to lead their child toward treatment, while they work to establish an environment that would be suitable for treatment. To support this, one could cite practical reasons—the earlier the person in withdrawal starts clinical consultations, the better. More and more time is wasted every day the family wavers back and forth, wondering whether or not they should take their child to get treatment. It is not at all unusual that as time goes by, the state of withdrawal grows worse, and the situation develops to the point that the only way to get the person in withdrawal to the clinic is to drag him or her there by force. This kind of waffling back and forth is clearly meaningless and, in fact, often harmful. Even if the person in withdrawal does not necessarily desire it, the parents should not hesitate to set out and seek treatment on their own while appealing to their child to go with them. There is no need whatsoever to hesitate on this first step.

Why is it so necessary to provide treatment to people in withdrawal? The sociologist Talcott Parsons once said the following: the sick person has the right to take off work and to receive treatment, but at the same time, the responsibility of the sick person is to try to heal and to cooperate with the therapist providing treatment. If it is the responsibility of a healthy adult to work, then the responsibility of the sick adult is to make efforts to get better. This helps us arrive at some simple yet secure conclusions about the perspectives we should use in treating the patient. I realize that readers might criticize me as being of the "treatment philosophy"—the notion that psychoanalysis is necessarily the best way to go. As a practicing psychiatrist, my belief in the value of psychoanalysis guides me in working with many patients in social withdrawal. I have never had any reason to believe that I should change this fundamental stance.

In this part of the book dedicated to practice, I write as concretely as possible from my perspective as a psychiatrist about methods to deal effectively with people in social withdrawal. Treatment is an important part of dealing with problems of adolescence, but at the same time, it is no exaggeration to say that more than half of the issue has to do with the attitude that the family adopts. In other words, if the family is simply aware of the most appropriate means of handling the situation, then it is possible to significantly alleviate the suffering of the child.

Recently, I have started conducting consultations with families via telephone and letter. The reason has to do with exactly what I have just been saying. Many families are in pain because they do not have any idea how to respond the problem facing them. If someone explains clearly how they should go about dealing with the issue, then the situation becomes more stable for the family. By making connections and working with a specialist, the family can begin dealing with the tenacious problem of withdrawal, and that alone goes halfway to solving the problem.

As result, I plan to use these pages to reveal all of the know-how that I have accumulated over ten years of experience. I have written the following chapter in the hope that if these suggestions are sufficiently put into practice, then the person in withdrawal will take a turn for the better.

I have not provided detailed statistics in this book about how successful treatment will be. It would be easy for me to cook up some rates of success, but they would be neither persuasive nor concrete. Likewise, I realize that if I bring in actual examples, it might help readers sympathize and feel at greater ease, but I am rather afraid that emotional responses will cloud the calm judgment of my readers. Of course, my methods are supported by many examples of patients who have experienced vast improvements, but I want to avoid seducing my readers with actual examples. Rather than impetuously seek to put my readers' minds at ease, I would prefer that my readers first recognize and attempt to understand the problem intellectually, even if they are still skeptical.

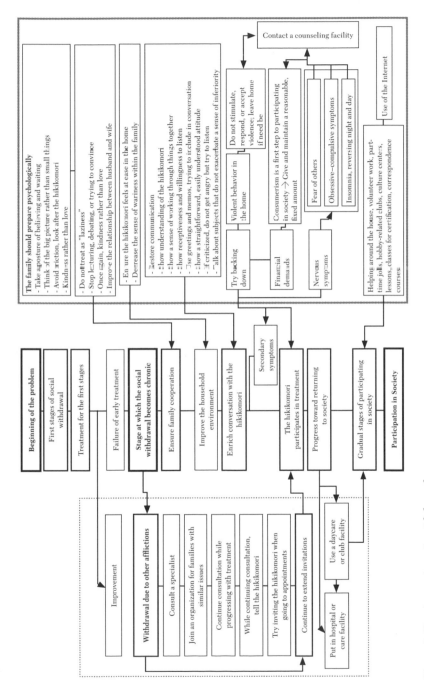

Figure 3. Treating patients in withdrawal.

I have summarized the contents of this half of the book on issues of practice in a flowchart that maps out ways to deal with withdrawal (Figure 3). As you read the following chapters, it may be easier to get an overall perspective of the contents by referring to the flowchart from time to time.

7 | IMPORTANT INFORMATION FOR THE FAMILY

There Is No "Wonder Drug"

One thing that I can say for sure about dealing with social withdrawal is that by the time the patients are brought in for consultations, they are usually in a rather bad state already. Once the patient's state has deteriorated past a certain point, it does not matter how hard the family works; it will be difficult for them to produce changes for the better. In fact, if anything, attempts to improve the situation usually just drive the person in withdrawal farther into a corner.

Consequently, the first thing that we need the family to understand is that there is no "wonder drug" that will cure the situation in a short amount of time. There is nothing for the family to do but to steel their resolve and realize that it will take time for their son or daughter to get better. One occasionally hears stories about patients suddenly recovering through a combination of effort, on the part of both the patient and the family, plus appropriate advice. I cannot say that is absolutely impossible, but in my experience, it is extremely atypical. If it were possible to solve withdrawal through effort alone, I think there would be many people for whom withdrawal was just a passing phase. In general, it takes between six months and two to three years, perhaps even more, to recover from a withdrawn state—and even then, of course, I am only talking about cases in which people get appropriate treatment.

In treating withdrawal, the question of how long the family can wait for the child to recover has a large bearing on how the recovery will proceed. Withdrawal begins with adolescence, and maturation can take some time. For that reason, it is necessary to have the family be patient as they wait for the child to reach full maturation. Impatience does not do any good at all. If anything, chronic impatience will just strengthen what I have described as the hikikomori system.

If the family can wait and still maintain hope, their attitude will influence the patient in desirable ways. Waiting involves adopting a cool and clear-headed posture vis-à-vis the situation. The family should not vacillate between joy and sadness at every little word and deed, nor should they hang on the slightest changes in the patient's situation. Instead, they should take a long-term outlook and behave in a level-headed manner. One reason the family should consult with a specialist is to help them adopt this kind of outlook. Meeting with a therapist will help them understand two things: first, that withdrawal is not something that is easily cured, and second, if everyone gives the treatment enough time and dedication, the patient will certainly recover. It sometimes happens during treatment that the patient will suddenly get a lot more active for no apparent reason and will show a greater desire to do things. One should not welcome this with blind optimism and simply assume that the patient has finally woken up and seen the light. This is because sudden changes in personality that occur in adolescence can often signal the beginning of some sort of psychological ailment. Even if there is some sort of change that looks at first glance like it might be for the better, it is best to pay plenty of attention, especially if the reason and direction of the change are unclear.

Of course, I do not mean that the family should just sit back and wait passively. Even as the family waits for changes to take place, they will need to make constant effort, which might not necessarily be obvious to the casual observers. It is necessary for the family to play their own part—they may have to adjust their own opinions or go for counseling sessions on their own. At the same time, it is important for them to determine exactly what it was that their child in withdrawal was trying to convey through his or her symptoms. It is important that the family holds back from meddling in ways that might be perceived as mean; instead, they must continue to watch over their child in a warm and caring way. One of my older colleagues once said to me, "Don't give a hand, give an eye," meaning "do not meddle in their affairs; just watch over them." No doubt this is exactly what families should be doing.

The Difficulty of "Love" in Treatment

In clinical situations, families who are going through rough times are often advised to hold on and "cherish their feelings of love" for the patient. In my opinion, however, the word *love* is an extremely difficult word. I am not trying to deny that love is a wonderful thing. It is wonderful when it happens to be there, but in the clinical situation, it is not something that can be controlled. There have been times that I, like many other psychiatrists, have said, "Now, touch one another with love," but the results always feel somewhat empty. No doubt that is because love cannot be forced.

But love is not something that the clinician should avoid, is it? Indeed, love is not to be avoided. Without it, treatment would be flat and passionless. Ultimately, is there some way to provide treatment without forcing love but without spoiling it as well?

I was once reading a book by Kurt Vonnegut, an American novelist who was popular during the 1980s, and I came across a quote that ran something like this, "Even if love loses, kindness will win." Although the exact wording escapes me, I remember the gist of this passage. I have some doubts about it. When he says "win," what will kindness win over? Is kindness always necessarily a good thing? Even so, there is still a certain truth in this passage. I would like to offer these words of encouragement to those families who have someone in withdrawal living in their midst.

The Close Bond of Love between Mother and Child

According to psychoanalytic theory, love has its fundamental roots in self-love. One cannot love others more than one loves oneself. Those who insist that they can are narcissists lacking self-awareness. That is what psychoanalysis teaches us. Love for the family is similar. If anything, the fact that it is sometimes difficult to distinguish between love and self-love means that we should pay more attention to love within the family. Often, love within the family is linked with a desire to possess the other people and control them, and this becomes the reason for occasional outbursts of virulent criticism. Later, I discuss violent outbursts in the household, but those too are a product of love. After a violent rage, sometimes the parties will apologize profusely to one another; the child will try to show his or her thoughtfulness, and the mother will hold the child in an embrace that goes on and on—it seems that the thing that lies behind such tragic forms of "love" is a loss of distance and control. "Love" that is "blind" simply makes treatment all the more difficult. In such cases, people are making the simple mistake of believing that "love" means unequivocal support for the ailing family member. Let me give an extreme example. There are times that a mother will refuse to listen to the therapist and ignore what he or she has to say, simply because the mother sees the therapist as an interloper trying to interfere in the love between mother and child. This kind of intense bond of love simply aggravates the situation all the more and makes it all the more unstable. This kind of relationship is called a "symbiotic relationship." The parent tries with all his or her might to calm the child's mind through strong feelings of love; however, the more energy the parent puts into it, the more that affects the child's demands and condition, often leaving the child in a state of exhaustion.

Of course, individuals in withdrawal also have a strong desire to be loved and thought of as necessary. At the same time, however, they are unable to rid themselves of the sense that they are disposable and might be abandoned at some point. The more efforts the mother makes, the more hikikomori individuals feel that they are weaklings who cannot exist without their own mother. They realize they do not know how to function if their mother were to abandon them. I have heard patients in their twenties and thirties say this over and over again. This just goes to show that these patients are "little boys and little girls" in the bodies of adults. Contrary to the mother's intentions, her selfless dedication does not save her child from this fear; it only amplifies it.

The Problem of Codependence

In psychiatry there is a word *codependence*. Originally, it was used to indicate the kinds of family relationships one finds in families with a member suffering from alcoholism, but nowadays, it is used in a somewhat broader sense than just that. The family of an alcoholic, most often the wife, suffers a great deal of worry because of the husband's drinking habits and the violence that accompanies his drunkenness; however, as that kind of relationship continues over the years, it becomes increasingly difficult for the wife to leave her husband, even though she is constantly being put in difficult situations. Wives in these situations often find their self-worth in playing the role of the supportive wife who takes care of an alcoholic husband. Meanwhile, the husband relies on his wife who continues to do things for him, and although the wife usually seems to be extremely upset on the surface, she becomes invested in her own self-image as someone who takes care of a lousy husband. This kind of relationship is called "codependent." This is not a stable, reciprocal relationship in which people agree "I carry you, and you carry me." This is a relationship in which A supports B, and B uses A as a tool for his own satisfaction, and as a result it is one-sided and unstable.

Let's try substituting the words *person in withdrawal* for *alcoholic.* In the cases involving withdrawal, one often sees codependence in the mother–child relationship. If the mother–child relationship appears to be tight, then it is important to think about the relationship from this standpoint and try to determine whether the relationship is codependent. If it is, then the mother should ask herself whether she can get along with a different sort of relationship. Simply by looking at the problem from that standpoint, it sometimes becomes clear how to change the warped relationships and improve the quality of the connection.

Nearly 100 percent of the cases that I have seen that involve a codependent relationship with the mother also involve a dislike for and refusal to engage in relationships with other people. Because the patient is so strong in his or her refusal to engage with others, many mothers find themselves feeling, almost before they know it, as if they *need* to do their child's bidding. The mother, however, should not compromise herself. This is the main point of having the parents participate in treatment and counseling. The therapist should drive a wedge between the overly close bond between mother and child. At first, children in withdrawal will find this extremely disagreeable. It only makes sense that they should hate it that some outsider who has no relationship with the family should be talking with them. There are sometimes cases when the hikikomori patient will begin to throw a temper tantrum when the parents start to go to the clinic; however, in the cases that I have been involved with, if the parents respond in a resolute manner, this kind of resistance will not continue for long. If anything, it is more often the case that patients feel some relief when the parents begin to go to a clinic. I think that is because they find themselves relieved that the door to their secretive room has come open and the relationship with their parents has started to come into focus.

The Importance of Others as Mirrors

Once a fixed relationship has been established with society, then the parents' love will begin to take on meaning. What do I mean by that? A few moments ago, I stated that all love is self-love. I am not trying to argue about whether this is true; if anything, it seems that when one looks at love, this is the only explanation that makes any sense. If we accept this hypothesis, then why don't all people behave in narcissistic, self-involved ways? I believe that the answer has to do with the functions of society. What I am trying to say is that in order to maintain this thing known as self-love, it is necessary to have what I call "the mirror of the other." The best possible situation is that one preserves one's love for oneself by loving other people or by receiving the love of others.

Young people who are in a withdrawn state, however, do not have that sort of mirror. All that they have is an empty mirror that never reflects anything but their own face. That kind of mirror is not helpful in producing an objective view of the self. No sooner do they see an omnipotent image of themselves—a self that seems to be brimming with power and possibility—than that image suddenly disappears, only to be replaced by a miserable image of themselves as people who have no value and no reason to live. Their mirrors produce only extremely unstable, warped images of themselves. In other words, it is necessary for them to use the "power" of someone outside the family to stabilize their "mirrors" and maintain a healthy (and by that I mean "stable") sense of self-love.

It is impossible for people to go on living without a sense of self-love. For self-love to function properly, one needs an appropriate circuit through which one can circulate. Through childhood, the interactions that take place in the circuit between the self and the family are enough, but once the individual becomes an adolescent, the situation changes. What changes the situation above all else are the changes the child experiences in sexual desire. Indeed, during and after adolescence, it is hard to love oneself without the mediation of love for the opposite sex. This kind of heterosexual love is not at all something the family can provide.

"Kindness" over "Love"

This is not merely a logical argument without any grounding in reality. I have seen over and over again that a relationship with the opposite sex can be the beginning of a cure for many hikikomori young men. Conversely, the biggest barrier for young men who are having trouble getting over their withdrawn state is their inability to forge a relationship with the opposite sex. Of course, a relationship with the opposite sex cannot be provided as a part of therapy. And yes, here as well, love works only when it comes about by chance.

For those reasons, one should not necessarily rely on love during therapy. Rather, if not love, the family should make every endeavor to give the patient kindness. Kindness is not something that comes about without sympathy, but it is this very sympathy that the person in withdrawal seeks out. Interacting with kindness, deep sympathy, a considerate attitude—this is the attitude that we should adopt in treating a person in withdrawal. The stronger the expressions of love, the more likely it is to bring about a censorious reaction. In kindness, one does not find severe love–hate tendencies. It is ideal for the family to adopt an attitude of kindness that is grounded in intellectual understanding and emotional sympathy.

8 | THE GENERAL PROGRESS OF TREATMENT

What Is the Final Goal?

Earlier in the book, I wrote about the hikikomori system in which the systems of individual, family, and society have lost contact with one another. Such systems involve a kind of vicious circle, and the worse it gets, the more likely it is that the withdrawn state will stabilize and become chronic. It does not just hold the individual captive. As the individual takes shelter from the social body, it holds both the individual and the family in its grasp. The family are also drawn deeply into the hikikomori system.

There are various advantages to thinking about social withdrawal as a system, but probably one of the biggest is that it allows us to schematize it in a way that can explain the problems and the progress of treatment. This schema helps us answer a number of questions. Where do the problematic points lie? Are they in the individual, the family, society, or in the points of connection between all three? What parts should we work on to disengage the system from its vicious cycle? Thinking about withdrawal in a schematic way helps us explain these things in an easily understandable fashion.

Figure 4 is effective in helping evaluate how far the current level of treatment has progressed. For instance, there is a stair-step pattern in terms of the relationships between the three systems. There is a state in which the individual avoids the family and the family is not participating in treatment. There is a state in which the family is coming for consultation but they are not telling the individual. There is a state in which the family is going for consultation but, although the individual knows that, he or she cannot (or will not) come to be seen by the therapist. There is a state in which the individual is coming for treatment but the family is refusing treatment. It is useful to attempt to organize these states and view them in terms of patterns.

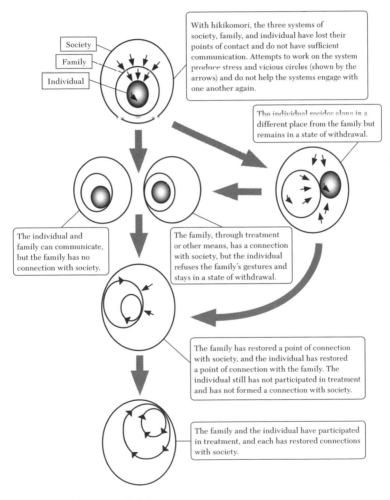

With hikikomori, the three systems of society, family, and individual have lost their points of contact and do not have sufficient communication. Attempts to work on the system produce stress and vicious circles (shown by the arrows) and do not help the systems engage with one another again.

The individual resides alone in a different place from the family but remains in a state of withdrawal.

The individual and family can communicate, but the family has no connection with society.

The family, through treatment or other means, has a connection with society, but the individual refuses the family's gestures and stays in a state of withdrawal.

The family has restored a point of connection with society, and the individual has restored a point of connection with the family. The individual still has not participated in treatment and has not formed a connection with society.

The family and the individual have participated in treatment, and each has restored connections with society.

Society

Family

Individual

Figure 4. Changes in a hikikomori system.

The thing that I am aiming for in the short run through therapy and consultations is the following: a state in which the family and the individual both participate in uninterrupted treatment and in which the family can also talk in level-headed ways about the treatment. In my experience, if the therapist can help the individual and family get to this state, it is just a matter of time before the individual is able to recover. At the very least, the situation will begin to improve, and the hikikomori system will begin to be disengaged.

Conversely, if all the parties have made continual efforts toward treatment but the individual still has trouble participating in society, then there is some kind of problem in the flow of communication surrounding the treatment. If even a single person in the family feels negatively about the treatment, it can cause a big roadblock. It can also be problematic if the family is overly zealous about treatment. For instance, overzealousness can be a problem if the family becomes impatient and they run all over, looking for better treatment than what they are receiving, and jumping from one hospital or therapist to the next. Overzealousness can also be a problem when the family dedicates themselves to an excessive degree to family activities or to their own individual counseling. In those two cases, the family is completely leaving the child's intentions behind. When confronted by a submissive response from the child, such families tend to think, "We've been making all of this effort, so why doesn't our child respond?" Unless it is possible to restore reciprocal communication between the individual and the family, it is not possible to treat a person in withdrawal successfully. It is not especially easy to reach the goal for treatment that I laid out just a few moments ago. I am not simply being pessimistic. If anything, I am trying to emphasize the facts— namely, if one puts in a specific kind of effort in a continuous, tenacious fashion, that effort will inevitably pay off.

Two Steps for Recovery

Let me discuss the general process of treatment. I have outlined my thoughts about how it should progress in Figure 4, which shows the changes in a hikikomori system over the course of counseling.

What steps are involved in trying to help a person recover from a chronic state of withdrawal? At the most basic level, there are two big steps. The first is to attempt to restore the point of connection with the two neighboring systems. In other words, it is necessary to restore a point of connection between the individual and the family, and between the family and society. Once that has happened, then it will be time for the second big step: restoring the point of connection between the individual and society.

When I write about these steps like this, they seem self-explanatory and obvious, but contrary to what one might expect, in reality, people often do not follow the order that I have just given. One often sees families trying to forge a relationship between the individual and the social system but failing in the process. One example would be when families force their children to attend a boarding school out in the provinces somewhere. Sometimes families rent an apartment and force their child to live out of the household on their own. There are other times when families find a live-in working position for their child, then force him or her to take the job. In such situations, it may seem that the individual is on the right track, but before long, the individual will get worn down and fail, leaving only a lingering distrust of the family. The most certain route to avoid repeating those mistakes is to go about restoring the point of connection with the neighboring systems.

It is relatively easy to get the family system and the social system working in conjunction with one another. In concrete terms, this is what happens when the parents begin going to a counseling center for treatment or participating in meetings with the extended family. A family should not try to handle withdrawal within the immediate family alone; they should take an open attitude and think about establishing a broader connection with society.

The Role of the Parents Is Most Important

The next thing to deal with is how to get the family system and the individual system to work together. The big question is this: in what way can the individual in withdrawal and the family restore a point of connection? To put it concretely, this is the stage at which conversations between the individual and family become possible and the family works to establish a closer, more candid exchange with the hikikomori child. In my experience, this is the stage that is most difficult and that takes the greatest amount of time. Children in a chronic state of withdrawal avoid even having to *see* the members of their family. Sometimes they do not speak at all and instead convey their thoughts by writing them on notes. Still, treatment will not progress properly if the family tries to skip this stage, no matter how deep the state of isolation. Conversely, the care we pay to this stage greatly determines the future progress of healing. That is how important this stage is.

The reason this stage is so difficult goes beyond the fact that the problem involves the relationship between the individual and the family. In receiving therapy, differences between the value systems of the various members of the family become an issue, along with the friction those differences cause. For instance, one often sees cases where the mother is the only one who is zealous about the treatment while the father and siblings do not show much interest, thus inviting the criticism that they are "lazy." Of course, there also cases where the roles are reversed.

It is worth emphasizing once again that when working to disengage a hikikomori system, the parents play the most important role. It is not possible to expect a sufficient recovery unless both parents work together in a cooperative fashion. (One can make exceptions for families who have lost one parent through death or divorce.) I remember one case in which the older sister of a young man in withdrawal was the only one who was worried, whereas the parents just spent all of their time yelling and trying to spur him to action. Inevitably, it was only the sister who came to the clinic. I said to her, "It usually isn't especially helpful for therapy if only the siblings get involved—or at least, it isn't helpful for him. You shouldn't be coming to counseling for your brother. If anything, you should be thinking about your future and doing what you can to further that." The sister took my advice and after that, she stopped cooperating in the treatment for her brother altogether. As a result, the parents had no choice but to come themselves. It was a small step, but it was one in the right direction. The doctor administering the therapy has no choice but to engage in a continual, concerted series of negotiations, helping everyone make one small step after another on the path to recovery.

When there are significant differences within the family, it is first necessary to make sure that, at least to a certain extent, the whole family is willing to cooperate before trying to engage the child in communication. The reason I say "to a certain extent" is that we cannot expect that everyone will be on the exactly same page all the time. Also, there is a tendency on the part of the parents to get more enthusiastic about the therapy once it seems to be proceeding along the right track. It is best that everyone begins treatment with three major understandings: (1) being in withdrawal is not the same as being "lazy," (2) treatment is a necessary condition for recovery, and (3) the cooperation of the family is also necessary.

If there is too much discord between the parents and the two are unable to reach a shared consensus despite their best efforts, then I recommend that they go to couples' counseling before starting on a course of treatment with their child. It is important that the parents not be afraid of change and show their willingness to deal with difficult problems. A change in attitude will certainly make itself felt to their child and should help bring about positive results.

Do Not Think of Withdrawal as "Laziness"

Once the family is on the same page and has adopted the kind of attitude I have described above, what steps should they take to deal with their son or daughter? Previously, I recommended that the family takes one step at a time in their attempts to deal with their child. That is because, if one tries suddenly to introduce a point of contact into a hikikomori system—in other words, if one tries to force communication—then it often just seems that the family is being mean and trying to prod their child. It is first necessary to sufficiently adjust the family environment, and then gradually soften the "protective walls" that surround the withdrawn child and separate him or her from the rest of the family.

The family's measures should move forward incrementally based on changes in the condition of the withdrawn child. I say this because at first, children in withdrawal will ordinarily refuse all efforts from everyone around them. The first task for the family is to take the time to soften the child's resistance, a little at a time. As a result, the first goal is to *stabilize the feelings of the child within the household.*

Most withdrawn people have hardly any friends and do not go outside for long periods of time. In other words, the household is the only place where they feel like they belong. It is necessary to make them at least feel that they are at ease and can relax in the home. This is an essential prerequisite for moving forward and working on recovering a position in society. For this to happen, it is necessary to realize that the son or daughter is not simply being "lazy."

It is hard to see all the worries and conflicts that withdrawn children experience in the household; there is a tendency to think they are just frittering away all their time living a carefree existence. It is often the case, however, that the family members cannot even imagine the feelings of inferiority, discouragement, and inadequacy the child is experiencing.

I explained before that yelling and trying to scold a person into action are harmful, but what people think of as "well-reasoned arguments" are also not very helpful. Here are several of the kinds of arguments I am talking about. "You've got a responsibility to go out and work once you're past twenty." "People who don't work don't deserve to eat." "We spoiled you so that's why you turned out this way. We're not spoiling you anymore." "You're at the age where you can earn your own money, so we're not giving you any more allowance." "Unless we treat you strictly, you're never going to make anything of yourself."

All of these are the kinds of things one would expect upright and decent people to say. None of these arguments is completely off the mark. These words are all correct—too correct perhaps—and in reality, all they do is make the person in withdrawal more embarrassed and wound him or her all the more. As Nakai Hisao has pointed out, in psychiatric cases involving adolescents, it is especially necessary to try to avoid making them feel embarrassed. If one berates them for being "lazy" or tries to plead with them using "well-reasoned arguments," they will only feel that they are being driven farther into the corner. Telling them they are "spoiled," "selfish," or "self-centered" just does the same thing. It goes without saying that driving a person into the corner does not help him or her get better.

The Most Anxious Person Is the One in Withdrawal

All of that being said, the family is often still not able to put their anxieties to rest. For instance, I often hear the concern "if my child feels too comfortable in the household, then he won't want to leave and go outside into the real world, will he?" This makes sense, but to tell the truth, family members will ask that question only when they do not sufficiently understand their son's or daughter's feelings.

What we need to understand is that no one fears getting stuck in a state of withdrawal more than the person who is in withdrawal. I suspect that holds true for just about every hikikomori case. No matter how at home they feel in the household, they are experiencing feelings of anxiety that will not go away.

The point is that the family's worries are the same worries the withdrawn person is also experiencing. Even though the parent might think, "Children have no idea how much their parents love them," the child often shares the same set of values, more than the family ever realizes. One reason the family's sermons and "well-reasoned arguments" do not seem to reach the child is precisely because of this. Almost everyone grows unhappy when others begin lecturing them about what they already know, and it makes them want to argue back.

People in withdrawal also feel anxiety about the future and regret their current situation but simply do not know how to fix it. They are not spending their time just lounging carefree around the house, doing whatever they feel like. They are disappointed in themselves but also feel unable to go out into society. Before anything else can be done, it is important for the family to understand that and show sympathy.

Restoring a Trusting Relationship with the Family

In the second step, the main task is to gradually increase the number of opportunities for conversation with the person in withdrawal, and thus reestablish a trusting relationship with the family. In situations involving withdrawal, conversations between the child and the other family members are often extremely impoverished. It is not uncommon for families to say that apart from some occasional preaching, they have no idea what to say to their son or daughter. But the longer that state of impoverished conversation continues, the more damaged the relationship within the family will become, thus making it increasingly difficult to start treatment.

I recommend to the family that they make a regular effort to try to talk to the child while making sure they do not get long-winded in the process. It is important not to give up and to keep trying over and over, working at it persistently. If there is no response forthcoming, do not try to force one. Start with regular greetings around the house and other small talk. If the child responds, then the family should increase the range of topics little by little. Small talk about things that are happening and things that are interesting to the child works best. Talking about work, school, peers, marriages, and other such things merely makes the child feel increasingly inferior and inadequate, so it is best to avoid those topics; however, if the child broaches those subjects, it is OK to talk about them. In fact, that is perhaps the one exception when one should feel free to talk about those topics. I touch on this in more detail later, but when the child starts a conversation, take it as an important opportunity. In such situations, the family should do their best to lend an ear, no matter what the topic of conversation might be.

When the child starts talking, it is also important to pay attention to his or her expressions and tone of voice. It does not matter how carefully the family chooses their words; it does no good to make a sour face or speak in words that are cold or formal. It is important to be careful to adopt an attitude that will make sense to the child. It is also important that the child does not sense any contradiction between the family's affect and their words. Family members should not try to convey what they want to say through affect and behavior; they should try to convey it with words. Of course, sarcasm or indirect attacks are strictly off-limits. The fundamentals for dealing with someone are to adopt "straightforward tactics" based on good faith. Circuitous or roundabout ways of attacking the child are not helpful in treatment. If anything, that just unnecessarily increases the child's suspicions about the family's ulterior motives and destabilizes the relationship with the household.

How Should the Family Accept Grudges and Criticism?

At the beginning, when the parents are making their first efforts at communication, there is usually no response or, more likely, their overtures are greeted with bewilderment; however, if they keep at it over time, then gradually, they will begin to get a response, and the child's attitude will begin to grow more flexible and pliant. As that happens, the conversations should gradually grow richer and more meaningful.

When the child begins to have more conversations with the family, the child will often say all sorts of unexpected things that cause the family consternation and bewilderment. For instance, it is sometimes the case that the child harbors some sort of secret "grudge" against the parents. As examples, he or she may say things like these.

- "The reason I'm so miserable right now is 'cause of you. You're my parents and you raised me this way, so you're responsible."

- "You forced me to go to school when I really didn't want to go."

- "If you had just put me in a special cram school back then so I could've prepared for college, then I wouldn't be this far behind right now."

- "You didn't even notice when everyone else was picking on me. You didn't have a clue what a hard time I was going through."

- "We were living in a horrible place back then, but you wouldn't let us move somewhere else."

- "I want to go back and redo middle school. I wish I could go back in time and do it all over again."

There are probably very few parents who can just sit back and listen calmly when their children are leveling attacks at them—attacks that the parents most likely see as unreasonable or even outrageous. The parents may find themselves wanting to argue back or justify themselves, saying things like "that's not true" or "that doesn't make any sense." What is important, however, is not who is right or wrong. What is critical is to let the child say what he or she wants without interrupting. Let the child get everything off his or her chest, and listen as he or she does it. The family should not interrupt the child right away and argue back, nor should they try to take control of the conversation by force and lead it in a different direction. Even when the child's memories are not accurate and he or she clearly has a mistaken understanding of what happened in the past, it is meaningful first to listen carefully to his or her feelings to see what sorts of thoughts have been troubling him or her.

Of course, there are many families who grumble, "Our child just keeps on saying the same kinds of things over and over, and we're fed up." However, those families are often not allowing their children to say all that they want to say. It is a rather difficult thing to be quiet and be a good listener, allowing a person who is in withdrawal to verbalize everything that they want to get off of their chest. What is important is *not* "what is right." What is important is to get a sufficient understanding of what sorts of things the child in withdrawal has been feeling. Even when the son or daughter has memories that are incorrect, it important to bear with them and listen in a way that will help them put those memories to rest. This is practically an inescapable ritual that any family must go through before any real communication can take place.

However, it is also necessary to realize that "lending an ear" and letting someone "twist you around their thumb" are two entirely different things. This may seem obvious, but there is often a tendency to mix these two things up. For instance, there are instances when the person in withdrawal gets so angry that he or she starts demanding an apology and perhaps even financial compensation. As a fundamental rule, the family should not give in to such demands. It is my supposition that such demands are usually leveled at families who are not willing to be bothered with the complaints of their child. The reason that people in withdrawal start resorting to strong language, wanting apologies or financial compensation, is so the family will listen to their complaints. What is important in the end is that the child feels "my family has lent me their ear and listened to my feelings." If it is possible to get the withdrawn child to feel that way, then sometimes the grudges and demands will gradually trail off, even if the family does nothing else.

What It Means to Be Truly "Receptive"

On one extreme, there are parents who respond to the criticism of their withdrawn children simply by rallying against them; on the other extreme, there are parents who take their children's criticism far too seriously. These parents find themselves overcome with deep regret, blaming themselves for the way they brought up their child and the environment they provided. This kind of thinking, however, is also a problem. Even if there are things the parents regret about the way they handled their child's development or education, dwelling too much on past regrets can provide obstacles to effective treatment. When I encounter such families, I give them this advice: "Don't be full of regret. Just reflect on what went wrong." If one reflects on what went wrong, it can help one think about appropriate measures if similar situations arise in the future. Excessive regret is not good because it leads families to behave in ways that are indecisive and thus ineffectual when they need to be responding in a resolute manner. Such parents end up apologizing and repeatedly making compensation, as if they were some sort of criminal. Such behavior is not helpful. Both the parents and the withdrawn child just end up growing increasingly confused.

To be truly "receptive," one has to be clear about where one is coming from. A receptive vessel is not bottomless—it is not a vessel without boundaries. That is not what being receptive means. A limitless, bottomless vessel simply makes the other person feel frightened that they will be swallowed up. To be receptive, it is necessary to have a "bottom" and a "framework," and if it looks like the vessel is going to get broken, one should respond resolutely to stave off that danger. Let me repeat the fundamental point—parents must show a "posture of receptivity" and, at the same time, a "receptive framework" that will be easy for the hikikomori child to understand.

Another thing that is necessary is for the family to be absolutely sure that they will continue with their efforts once they have started to engage the withdrawn child. At the beginning, all families are eager to help their children get treatment. They go to the hospital frequently; they do exactly what the doctor tells them to do; they participate in meetings for families of people like them; and they do their best to engage their son or daughter. However, when they find that the treatment takes a long time and that their child is not making rapid progress, many families grow apathetic. It is not unusual that families start off with a proper attitude but gradually stop what they need to be doing. And to tell the truth, quitting halfway is worse than doing nothing at all.

It may not be possible to tell from appearances alone, but hikiko-mori children are extremely sensitive to the changes in their families. They will certainly notice if their families begin reacting to them differently. That does not mean, however, they will immediately change in response to their families' wishes. If anything, they tend to look on rather coldly, trying to gauge how serious the family is about engaging with them and whether the family will behave in a fickle manner. When the family gives up on their efforts (usually after a concerted effort to start them), it is equivalent to the family saying, "We've given up on you again." To continue with treatment in the ideal way, first, the family must realize they need to proceed at a leisurely pace so the child does not feel stressed, and second, the family should be resigned to not giving up after six months or a year once they start to engage their child.

I have been saying all along that the final goal is to open up a route of healthy communication between the child and the family. What do I mean by that exactly? After observing many families, I believe one indicator of healthy communication is the ability for the parents and child to joke with one another. In other words, they share a relationship in which they can kid around in a natural way in the course of daily life. This sort of relationship gradually becomes possible when there has been a successful renegotiation of relationships within the family. For such a relationship to come about, there must be a moderate amount of distance, on the one hand, and a degree of familiarity, on the other. If there is *not* a sufficient degree of distance, then parents and children will not be able to joke with one another, and attempts to do so will lead to suspicions of "ulterior motives" or perhaps even violent outbursts. Conversely, when both parties are *too* reserved, it is not possible to make jokes. Once there is a moderate, stable degree of distance between the family and child, it becomes possible for everyone involved to start sharing views on how to cope with and overcome the withdrawal. Once that relationship is in place, it is easier for both parties to arrive at the ideal relationship for treatment.

The Problems of Playing the "Blame Game"

As I wrote above, the family must cooperate fully to treat a withdrawn child. The role of the family is far more important in treating cases of withdrawal than other afflictions. With other ailments, the patient is usually able to reach a certain level of improvement through the help of medicine or individual psychological counseling, even if the family does not cooperate fully. However, it is almost completely impossible to treat withdrawal without the cooperation of the family. Without the cooperation of the family, it is not possible to treat a hikikomori case if the child has no desire to get treatment or behaves in unstable, erratic ways.

To be more precise, when I say "family," what I am really talking about are the parents. The full involvement of the parents is essential for treatment. In fact, it is unnecessary and sometimes even harmful for other family members or relatives to get involved.

A lack of interest on the part of the father can sometimes be a problem, and in such cases the responsibility of treatment tends all too often to fall entirely to the mother. The situation works out better if the father entrusts everything entirely to the mother, but what usually happens is that the father occasionally starts scolding his child or tries spurring him or her on with a pep talk or shouting. The father usually thinks he is performing his paternal duty by behaving this way, but such behavior only inhibits the family's progress in treatment. Because fathers are typically tied up at work during the day, mothers usually cannot help but play a large role in their child's treatment. However, it has been my experience that the more passionate the father is about treatment, the easier it is for the child to make progress. In the end, it is preferable that both parents share a common understanding about how to help their child overcome withdrawal, and then put their energies together to make it happen. Even when it is difficult for everyone to go for regular, periodic counseling, the parents should make sure they are on the same page and share the same outlook when it comes to their child's treatment. It is sometimes possible to arrive at such consensus through family meetings, study groups, or other meetings.

Unfortunately, in cases of severe withdrawal, relationships between the parents are often in such a bad state that they are not able to communicate smoothly with each other. The father might blame it on the mother, insisting, "She was the one who bought up our kid wrong," while the mother might be equally unwilling to give up ground, blaming the problems on her husband by saying, "His lack of interest is the real reason for the problem." However, it is of utmost importance that the family avoids trying to find out who is "at fault." Such logic is counterproductive. That is right—asking who is "at fault" will never produce a clear answer, but it inflicts a huge amount of damage instead of helping in the process of healing. The one who is most susceptible to the "blame game" is the withdrawn child. When parents fight about who is at fault, it is easy for the child to begin thinking, "It's my parent's fault I'm like this," and that makes the situation all the worse.

It may seem like a roundabout way of improving the situation, but to avoid the blame game and making the situation worse, the parents must reconsider their own relationship as husband and wife. Sometimes a couple can solve these problems through talking with one another, but in some cases the couple may require counseling. In any case, for treatment to be effective, it is of utmost importance that the parents maintain a good relationship as husband and wife. Parents' willingness to deal with and solve their own discord, and thus overcome their own problems, is sure to give their children hope about their own situation. Moreover, as I have stated before, when there are problems in the family, mothers and their children often develop relationships that are cut off from the father, and that only impedes treatment. When the mother and father do have a close relationship, however, that prevents unhealthy, closed relationships from forming.

Staying in It for the Long Haul

Sometimes parents simply do not want to deal with the problem when their child is in severe withdrawal. In fact, the more severe the situation is, the more likely the parents are to feel that way. Such attitudes are especially common among fathers. One finds cases in which no matter how hard the mother tries, the father either will not respond or simply repeats, "You do something about it. I don't have a clue." The father may appear to be absorbed in work, but really, he is only avoiding the bigger problem by fleeing and taking refuge in work. In other words, the father is in his own state of "withdrawal." One has to criticize this sort of attitude as showing a lack of imagination. The real issue at hand is not the trivial question of who is to blame; the real issue is what should be done from that point forward to solve the problem. If the father does not take the initiative and act right away, he will still be saddled with the responsibility of continuing to take care of his own child ten or twenty years down the line, and by that time the child will be in his or her thirties or forties. That is right. . . . The child might still be his responsibility even after retirement. That is how severe the results will be if the father simply continues to be hands-off and ignores the problem staring him in the face.

There are certain parents who, when faced with the prospect of long-term difficulties, respond in an overly dramatic fashion, saying, "I'll do anything so that my child can get better—I'll make any sacrifice." That can also be a problem. It is important that the parents are sincere and honest about seeking out treatment, but parents should not throw away everything and give themselves over to treatment with single-minded devotion while ignoring everything else. Such behavior runs the danger of separating the treatment from the rest of the family's life, without allowing them to address important underlying issues.

Even so, many people, especially mothers, decide they are going to give up everything to take care of their hikikomori child, partly out of a feeling of atonement. I have already mentioned this several times, but an overly close relationship between mother and child tends, if anything, to impede the progress of treatment. Why is it then that such relationships develop so often? I believe it is because somewhere deep inside, both the child and the mother herself really want to create that sort of relationship. The sweet feeling of sacrificing oneself for one's child helps solidify an overly close relationship. In such cases, self-sacrifice and devotion become a kind of intoxicating poison. The withdrawn child begins to feel, "I cannot live without my mother," and that confirms to the mother, "my child cannot live without me." Of course, those feelings are really merely illusions, but the intoxicating effect of the poison is strong enough that both people begin to feel they cannot live without one another. I will say it once more: when one is trying to help a child get better, one should restrain oneself from practicing this kind of "love."

If the parents are serious about starting a long, concerted battle with the withdrawal—a battle that often ends up being somewhat of a war of attrition—the parents *must* be sure about their own positions as mother and father, each in their own individual world. The father typically has his duties at work and his associations outside the home, so what I am about to say is especially important for the mother. It is not desirable for her to spend twenty-four hours per day with the withdrawn child. The mother should make sure she has her own work—perhaps a part-time job—and hobbies. She should not give up lessons or things she is learning outside the home. She should not give up her interactions with people in society. Creating time for herself through those activities will help the mother maintain her own psychological balance. There are many cases in which the mother herself hates to leave the home and go outside, but if she makes up her mind and goes out, that will help the withdrawn child recognize her as an "individual." In other words, the child realizes that the mother has an individual existence separate from him or her and comes to accept this fact. That is an extremely important step in the healing process.

9 | IN DAILY LIFE

Starting Out by Speaking

Earlier in this book, I stated that approximately half of all people in withdrawal have extremely impoverished levels of conversation with their own family. I touched on this earlier, but in such cases, the first priority is to help reestablish conversation between the child and their family. In this section, I talk about concrete techniques for doing so.

If the child in withdrawal has stopped speaking, it is not uncommon that family members will not see him or her for months. In fact, that is not uncommon even in families where there is some level of communication. Nonetheless, even if the child manages to avoid his or her family altogether, there is no question that the child is secretly holding his or her breath and watching the family, never missing a thing. If the parents suddenly start talking to him or her, the child will of course notice immediately. He or she will think, "Oh, they're up to something," and start venturing guesses about different things that might happen. "Something must have put an idea into their heads. Maybe they read some special story in the newspaper about 'hikikomori.' I'll just sit back and watch to see how long their attention lasts." That is generally how the child will see them, and so the parents should be aware of this as they begin to interact with their child.

The best way to start out is with greetings. Try starting with simple things: "Good morning," "I'm heading out for a little bit," "I'm home," "Good to see you," "Bon appétit," "Thanks," "Good night," and so on. The family should not just say these things to their child. It will be more effective if they start saying these things to each other as well, taking advantage of every opportunity for communication. Of course, the withdrawn child will probably ignore these greetings, and at times he or she might even act annoyed; however, greetings never hurt anyone. It might seem a bit forced, but being careful to use these greetings at every opportunity is the first step. And it will seem tedious, but once the family has started using these greetings, the family should be sure not to let them die off and disappear.

There are cases when the child in withdrawal will say something to the family, even though the family has been saying nothing more than the usual greetings. This is a valuable opportunity to start a conversation, so the family should be sure not to let it slip by. The family should take every opportunity to get the child to speak, even if the conversation is not about anything of any importance. Even if the conversation is not really much of a conversation at all, the more opportunities there are for interaction, the more likely the withdrawn child will be to let down his or her guard with the family. If the child does not respond with even a single word of greeting, try using notes as well, but keep up with the greetings. As with the greetings, the content of the notes does not have to be anything important. Just one or two written sentences are enough. Questions like the following are probably safe: "What do you want with the rice tonight?" or "Is there anything you want me to pick up when I'm out today?" Ritualized greetings having to do with the season are fine as well, for instance, "The flowers in the garden are beautiful." If anything, it is probably best that the contents are as trivial and ordinary as possible to avoid causing undue agitation.

Often parents find that the conversation will take an unnatural direction or they will become too nervous to be able to say anything articulately; however, when one is talking to a child who has been holed up in the home for a long time, it still counts for something even if the conversation is awkward and unnatural. It does not matter even if the conversation seems forced or strange. The important thing is that the parents convey their desire to talk with their child and the fact that they are going to lengths to do so.

When talking to a child who is cooped up in his or her own room, it is important for the parents to talk from outside the room. It may be hard to believe, but some parents open the doors to their own child's room without knocking first. Other parents knock but go ahead and open the door without waiting for a response. Such behavior is not only counterproductive but goes against common sense. If it is still not possible to have a proper conversation, it is essential to be sure to show the maximum possible respect for the child's privacy. For that reason, it is best to speak to the child from outside the door without opening it.

How to Keep a Conversation Going

People often compare conversations to a game of catch. In other words, conversations are interactions that show a degree of reciprocity. An interaction that is not reciprocated is not much different than talking to oneself. In that sense, it is best not to talk in a condescending manner, thus indicating that one occupies a superior position. Likewise, it is best not to speak in a way that foists one's own conclusions onto the listener. If anything, it is best to be as vague and unobtrusive as possible. For instance, one should avoid saying, "The answer's such and such, for Christ's sake!" or "Everyone else in the world takes such and such for granted." Instead, it is better to talk in a fashion that is less presumptuous, such as, "I think probably the answer is such and such," or "Dad recommends such and such, but what do you think?" If one begins to feel comfortable with such expressions, it will lead to a deeper level of communication. Also, when calling out to the withdrawn child, it is best to avoid direct methods of address, such as the second-person pronouns *omae* or *kimi*, since they are more likely to offend the addressee.[1] I recommend speaking in a more polite fashion, calling the person by their name to which one should add the polite suffix *–san*. Simply saying *"kimi"* is not acceptable. Another possibility is the pronoun *anata*.[2]

Earlier in this book, I mentioned that it is best to avoid talking about the future as well as the child's friends of the same age; however, rather than making a comprehensive list of taboo topics, it is better to try to imagine life in the shoes of the hikikomori child. It is cruel to bring up talk about the future, marriage, or work to a person who feels that his or her life has been a failure and who is painfully aware of the fact that he or she has been so late in getting started in life. People in withdrawal even avoid remembering the fun that they had earlier in their lives. Even talking about TV stars who are about the same age can also cause pain. Probably the least difficult subjects have to do with current events or social issues. It is not unusual that young men in withdrawal have a high degree of interest in things that are going on in the world. Conversation does not have to be limited to that. If the child has some interest in something, then it is probably not a bad idea to ask questions about it.

Three Fundamental Rules about Finances

Money holds an incredibly important role for adolescents. There are some basic rules for how to handle money when dealing with adolescents in treatment—not just adolescents in withdrawal. They can be lumped together into the following three fundamental rules.

- Give a sufficient allowance.

- Decide on a fixed amount.

- Decide on the amount in consultation with the adolescent.

No doubt there are many parents who are uneasy with the first of these rules. No doubt, there are those who think that if one gives the withdrawn child enough money, that will do away with any desire to go out and get a job; however, one will realize that those fears are ungrounded if one has any real sympathy for the child. The reason that the child goes into withdrawal is not because he or she does not *want* to work but because he or she feels *unable* to work, even though he or she wants to.

Most families adopt an ad hoc, ill-advised policy of giving the child whatever money he or she wants whenever he or she wants it. There are two reasons that is dangerous. The first is that it makes it easy for the adolescent to squander the money. The other is that the child will gradually lose his or her desire for money. If the child begins to say, "There's nothing I really want so I don't need any money," that is an extremely bad sign.

When a person goes into withdrawal, that does not mean his or her capacity to feel desire has grown impoverished, but it is often the case that various types of desire—the desires for sex, things, and so on—do diminish. In the language of psychoanalysis, desire represents "the desires of the other." In other words, to a greater or lesser extent, the things that all of us want are determined by what others want. The values of things are determined by the extent of other people's desires for the same things, and for the most part, our desires reflect that value. That is the reason why we immediately begin to feel some regret when other people ask us for something we have gotten rid of. When one has less interaction with society, one feels at a greater remove from others. The greater the remove, the less desire one is likely to feel. If a person's desires grow very weak, then it becomes extremely difficult for him or her to return to their former state. Let me say it again—one should give the person in withdrawal a sufficient allowance. The reason is that this helps stimulate the desire for things and encourages the desire to participate in society through consumption. Needless to say, consumption does represent one method of participating in society, and in most cases of withdrawal, it represents the last remaining way for a patient to interact with society. It only makes sense that parents should not try to take that away.

Once a sufficient level of communication has been established, I believe it is important to make it clear exactly how much the child needs for living expenses. By this, I am referring to the total amount of money the child will spend on things that he or she likes, on things related to hobbies, on fashion, and on other things. To put it in a different way, I am referring to everything other than food and shelter. It is best for the family first to clarify the total amount those things would cost, then provide for those things in the form of an allowance of an agreed-on amount.

Often, when families actually sit down to ask withdrawn children how much they need, they will often respond with an amount that is unexpectedly and perhaps even unreasonably low. That reaction can be seen as a reflection of the child's inferiority complex or perhaps their gnawing sense that they have no real excuse for their actions. In my therapeutic experience, I do not remember ever encountering a case in which the family gave their child the chance to determine an allowance, and the child responded with an absurdly large amount of money. If the child does end up spending tens of thousands of yen each month, almost without exception the family adopts a strategy of giving only what the child wants at the time that he or she wants it. First and foremost, the goal is to get the person in withdrawal to use money in a planned fashion, so the family should discuss details with the child: "How much money do you need, and what for?" If the family is able to arrive at a figure, they are doing just fine. If the child has difficulty deciding on a figure, it is probably most realistic and persuasive for the family to figure out how much the child has spent on expenses during the last six to twelve months, calculate the amount spent per month, then use that to arrive at an amount for the allowance.

After deciding on an amount, it is important to stick to the agreement. If the child spends too much, the family can make him or her go without or can let him or her borrow against the next allowance. If the child goes out and gets a part-time job, then it is advisable to still continue giving the allowance, at least for a while. That is what I meant earlier when I wrote about deciding on something and sticking to it.

Sometimes money makes people lose their senses, but I believe that if used sensibly, money can also help bring a person back to his or her right mind. Use money, and it disappears. Do not use money, and one can save it. I cannot tell you how many cases I have seen in which people seem to lack common sense about those obvious principles. Maintaining the fundamental rules of finances means taking these principles to heart. Doing so will surely help the withdrawn person become increasingly aware of his or her own financial position.

How Should One Deal with "Reversion to Childhood"?

Several years ago, I came across a scene in a TV drama showing the problems of adolescence. The show depicted a son who threw violent fits in front of the other members of his family and the conflict he experienced with his mother. In the end, she accepted his feelings, realizing he was a young man only old enough for middle school, and held him to her breast and let him suckle at her nipples, almost as if he were a baby. When I saw that, I was astounded. How on earth could anyone construe that scene as some sort of happy ending? If anything, I became increasingly gloomy imagining what would happen next to the mother and son. There is no theory that might explain how such behavior might lead to healing. The drama just seemed to be a vulgar display of what people blindly *think* might lead to some sort of healing. It struck me that was not just a problem on the part of the screenplay writers or the director. It seemed to me that the problem lay with a society that wants that sort of resolution.

If the person in withdrawal is experiencing a state of regression or what is popularly called a "reversion to childhood," I cannot recommend a course of action like that depicted in the show I just described. There might be certain therapists who might recommend helping the child to revert even further as a way to "cure" the withdrawal, but experience has led me to oppose that recommendation.

Here, in a nutshell, is the logic used by those therapists who support encouraging the child to regress even further. Certain children are forced to be "good boys and girls" from the time they are very little. As a result, they have not ever really had the chance to be emotionally dependent on their parents in the way that a child might want and expect.[3] A certain amount of responsibility for this lies with the parents, who were unable to provide that relationship for their children. A state of withdrawal is a sign of desire to enter into a relationship of loving dependence, and so, the theory goes, one should respond to this desire in an unfaltering fashion. "Treatment" involves helping a patient through the maturation process all over again, and certain therapists say one should start giving unconditional love through skinship.

Of course, not of all of the logic I have just described is entirely wrong. I am not trying to say that it is. It can be helpful with certain kinds of preadolescent problems, as well as when a person is just beginning to skip school and go into withdrawal. In the therapeutic setting, however, this way of thinking, if anything, seems to be more harmful than not. I have suggested that acceptance needs to come with a framework, but this framework absolutely should *not* involve skinship. Accepting the emotional dependence of the patient must stop at the level of words. As a general rule, one should avoid combining emotional dependence with physical contact.

How to Deal with Obsessive Compulsion

Obsessive-compulsive behavior is like violent behavior in the household in that both draw the mother into the problem, and it is very easy for her to become the victim. Obsessive-compulsive behavior that involves checking on something over and over is especially exhausting in that it repeats until both the patient and the mother are exhausted. I can think of one case in which a patient had an obsessive fear of crematoriums. He happened to be in the car with his mother when they went near a funeral hall, and he became terribly ill. He forced his mother to drive back the way they had come, and they went back and forth dozens of times, until his mother was so exasperated and exhausted that she practically had a car accident. It is extremely difficult to handle such cases.

Obsessive-compulsive behavior generally arises from an obsessive-compulsive disorder, and so one should prioritize that in delivering treatment; however, when obsessive-compulsive behavior arises as a secondary symptom accompanying the state of withdrawal, the situation is probably quite different. My impression is that obsessive-compulsive behavior that arises as a secondary symptom is often a sign that there is a problem in communication. In such situations, if the parents continue to participate in therapy with their child and they begin to improve the quality of their communication, then the obsessive-compulsive behavior will improve. The person who is exhibiting the obsessive-compulsive behavior may be stubborn, but the family is also caught in a cycle and finds themselves unable to respond in a flexible way. First and foremost, it is necessary for the family to negotiate and try to get their child to work with them to fully understand the symptoms.

When the Person in Withdrawal Lives Alone

Sometimes people go into withdrawal while living away from their family for a long period of time, for instance, when they are in college.

There are also cases when hikikomori children are forced out of the family home so they can "learn to stand on their own two feet." Except in very exceptional cases, living on one's own does not help a person in withdrawal to become more independent. I say this because in most cases, they just end up becoming a shut-in in their own apartment. If anything, sending withdrawn children out to live on their own just causes more problems—it makes it harder to have meaningful interaction with the family and more difficult to enter into treatment. The son or daughter loses both physical and psychological contact with the family, and it becomes just about impossible to break out of what I have previously referred to as the hikikomori system.

As a general rule, when someone is living alone in a state of withdrawal, it is important to keep up the interactions until it becomes possible to bring him or her back to live with the family. However, if the family is too aggressive about forcing interaction, it is possible that the child might simply disappear all of the sudden one day. To avoid that, the family should take their time, and they should make numerous visits before trying to bring the child back into the household. If the child insists that he or she does not want to live with the family under any circumstances, the family should try, however minimally at least, to increase the amount of contact, perhaps by having him or her move to an apartment in the same neighborhood. It is also important to have an environment conducive to communication. Communication by telephone makes the most sense, and if it is possible to communicate via fax or e-mail, that can also work as well. The family can call on a periodic basis, can drop by the apartment directly, and can—if the child is willing to respond—invite him or her to the house to spend the night occasionally. In this way, the family can interact with the child in a way that moves step by step toward a life together.

Learning to Accept Laxity

It is often the case that as individuals slide into withdrawal, they become lax and disorganized in all aspects of their lives. First of all, the rhythms of their lives will become extremely disordered; for instance, they might sleep all day and spend all night awake. Another possibility is that the room where they are cooped up becomes extremely cluttered, so full of things and garbage that there is not even enough room to walk. Sometimes, when the room becomes too terrible, the child will begin to occupy other spaces in the house, such as the living room or the kitchen, placing video game software, videos, and magazines there in big stacks.

I often hear complaints that children in withdrawal "do nothing but watch TV cooped up in their own rooms" or "are always playing video games." There is a tendency to think badly of people who demonstrate the *otaku*-like, autistic tendency to show enthusiasm for only the things that interest them. There is an assumption that this tendency is necessarily pathological; however, in the case of withdrawal, it is, if anything, desirable that the person maintains an interest in society, even if it is only through the screen of a television. There is a strong-rooted assumption out there that if people get completely infatuated with television or spending time on the computer, it will only become harder for them to deal with the rest of the world, but that assumption is completely without foundation. Rather than jump the gun and act as if there were a crisis, it is better for the parents to spend time with the child and try to have fun. Just the very act of enjoying something together represents an excellent act of communication.

In any case, it is true that if one is just caught up in dealing with the surface elements of the withdrawn patient's life, such as his or her "attitude toward life," then the true nature of the problem will not become visible. The way to start engaging with people in withdrawal is simply to accept them as they are—slovenliness and all. The kind of slovenliness we are talking about arises as a secondary symptom of going into withdrawal, and so it does not make any sense to try to cure only that part of the problem.

Accepting a person's slovenliness is connected with respecting his or her privacy. First of all, one should be sure not to make intrusive incursions into the territory that the withdrawn child thinks of his or her own room. To put it in more grandiose terms, a person's room is his or her castle—a sacred territory. Parents should not go into the room on their own accord, clean the room, or empty the trash without being asked to. First and foremost, parents should make it clear that they respect the value that the room holds for their child. Parents can do this through some relatively small efforts. For instance, they might stop opening the door whenever they feel like it or call from outside the door whenever trying to start a conversation with their child. Another important way to show respect for the child's space is to be sure to talk with him or her ahead of time before cleaning the room. At the same time, the parent should make every effort not to allow the child to place his or her things in the communal spaces of the house, such as the living room, in order to make the boundaries of their privacy clear. If the child's things are already all over, then the family should be sure to negotiate in meaningful ways before having the child put the things away. That should also be done only after making "the framework of acceptance" clear.

Maintaining a Stable Environment Is the Most Important Thing

To treat a hikikomori patient, it is important to try to avoid as many big changes as possible to the patient's affiliations or to the family environment. In concrete terms, this means trying to avoid or postpone having the child officially drop out of school, quit work, or be transferred to a different job. One should also try to avoid or postpone changing residences, building a new house, and making other such changes to the home. When individuals feel that things are going profoundly wrong at school or at work, they are more likely to want to drop out of school or leave their employment officially; however, it is often the case that if the parents follow their children's wishes and complete the procedures necessary to do those things, the child suddenly loses even more energy and becomes increasingly despondent. The fact that people in withdrawal still have spots officially waiting at school or work for them places constant, silent pressure and stress on them. That is the reason they want to cut off their affiliations and feel better about themselves as quickly as possible. Still, when they actually do quit, the reality of not having any place in society becomes that much heavier and difficult to bear. Even if the child has no desire whatsoever to return to school, it is better to retain some official standing at school rather than abandon it altogether. If he or she begins to express that kind of desire to withdraw, the family should do their best to retain the position, even if that takes some convincing.

The same is true for changing residences. There are cases in which families have felt no choice but to move because their child is concerned about the gazes of the neighbors and wants to escape, but in the end, the change did not lead to any change in the withdrawn condition—if anything, it made it worse. There are a few reasons for this. It is often the case that hikikomori patients fall into the trap of thinking "I'm like this because I'm in a bad environment." The reality, however, is that they have become extremely sensitive to relationships and the gazes of others as a result of their withdrawn state, and that will not change if they simply move. To make matters worse, they begin to feel a strong sense of regret inside, thinking, "I've gone and caused my family a great deal of unnecessary trouble." This becomes a rift between them and the family, and the communication ends up suffering even more.

However, there are cases in which moving has proved to be a successful step. Things are more likely to go well if the move is made not just because the hikikomori child wants it but because the entire family comes to a shared consensus that moving is the right thing to do.

10 | THE SADNESS BEHIND VIOLENCE
IN THE HOUSEHOLD

Resigning Oneself and "Taking It" Is the Wrong Approach

A rather large percentage of cases of social withdrawal are accompanied by violent outbursts in the household, which just makes the problem of withdrawal that much more difficult to deal with. Explosions of violent behavior that come as the result of small things or perhaps without any reason whatsoever only make the atmosphere in the home bleaker and more desolate. Unnatural, tense silences begin to rule over the house, and the family is compelled to spend their days in fear, watching the withdrawn child's slightest expressions and gestures.

It is especially easy for the mother to become the victim of these violent outbursts. It is often the case that, if one were to judge just on outward appearances, the mother seems to have been treated like a slave for years on end. It is no exaggeration to say that in this situation, the mother and child live their lives stuck to one another for twenty-four hours a day, robbing her of even the ability to get a good night's sleep. A mother might be awakened at any hour as her child suddenly recalls some grudge from long ago and forces her to listen to it for hours on end, completely disregarding the time of night. Even so, the child might not approve of the mother's tone of voice and fly into a groundless fit of rage.

There are some specialists in adolescent issues who would advise parents to resign themselves and take it. The reasoning is that once the child is satisfied, he or she will settle down; by exposing the parent to a violent outburst, the child has turned the tables and made the parent into a child. From the point of view of the therapist, however, it is simply mistaken to try to deal with the problem this way. In fact, it is not only a mistake, but it sometimes helps prolong the violent outbursts. That is because exposing oneself to angry behavior simply becomes a dangerous provocation.

I say more about this later, but the thing that is at the bottom of these violent outbursts is sadness. If they came out of just a simple outburst of feelings, no doubt they would just get over it and move on; however, violent behavior almost never ends this easily. The perpetrators feel so wounded that they end up turning to violent behavior, but at the same time, they have a hard time forgiving themselves. On the other hand, they feel that it was their parents who created a "self that cannot be forgiven." Violent behavior involves a vicious circle of self-reproach and blame.

The view that the parents did something bad enough to bring about violence is merely the kind of "hunt for the bad guy" logic that can lead to mistaken diagnoses like the belief that the mother was the cause of the disease—something people would say about certain mental disturbances in the past. This leads me to something intriguing that I have noticed. In cases of social withdrawal and domestic violence that I have observed, there have been almost no instances of people who suffered abuse as a young child, at least in the real clinical and legal sense of the term *abuse*. Of course, this is nothing but my empirical impression gathered from the consultation room, so I am not quite sure if one can draw general conclusions from this, but from my experience treating victims of childhood abuse, I can guess at the general reasons. People who have experienced severe abuse begin to show signs of dissociative personality disorder (also known more colloquially as "multiple personality disorder") or post-traumatic stress disorder; however, it is often the case that this is does not turn into a desire to engage in "revenge against the parents" through more domestic violence. If anything, it is more likely that victims of abuse start behaving violently toward their own wives and children later in life when they create their own families.

In the earlier chapter about how to talk to children in withdrawal, I wrote about how to deal with grievances from the past, so I will not repeat myself here. I just emphasize that it is important to listen to the grievances, treating them as words, while making sure that they do not get the better of you.

What It Means to "Reject Violent Behavior"

My fundamental stance is that it is critical to reject violence. I mean that one should reject violence altogether as a method—whether it be doling out legitimate corporal punishment or the understandable desire to engage in revenge. When I say that I reject violence "as a method," I mean that even if one is systematically against corporal punishment, there are times that one is compelled to break with that and recognize the utility of corporal punishment, but that is another story altogether.

When I say "reject," of course, I do not mean that one should have a standoff and engage in a duel of sorts. Standoffs only prolong the violent outbursts. Rejecting violence also means rejecting "violence for the sake of suppressing violence." Attempts to suppress household violence through force are almost sure to fail. There is a bit of folk wisdom that violence just leads to more violence. It is worth taking note of that here.

The only way to deal with violent outbursts at home is to face them while rejecting them. This much is clear; however, there are many different ways that one might "reject" violent behavior, depending on the situation.

The thing that determines its severity and the difficulty in dealing with violent outbursts with it is not the content of violence. If anything, it is the length of time that the outbursts have been continuing. If the violent outbursts have been going on for just a few weeks, then they are relatively easy to treat, even if the violent behavior is quite severe. On the other hand, it can be quite difficult to treat chronic outbursts of violent behavior if they have been going on for years, even if the violence itself is not all that dramatic. Below I provide sections with concrete discussion about how to deal with two broad categories of violent behavior: "violent outbursts in their early stages," which prove less difficult to deal with, and "chronic bursts of violence," which have continued for a long time and are therefore a bigger problem.

A Sadness That Cannot Be Shouldered by One Person Alone

Regardless of how one deals with the problem, it is absolutely essential that one begin by sufficiently understanding what is behind the violent outbursts. But how is one to make sense of a person's feelings when he or she feels that there is no option but to behave in a violent fashion?

It does not matter what the objective truth happens to be; people who engage in such behavior have a strong sense that their lives up until that point have been full of misery. They see their history as a series of failures—they may feel that they failed at their entrance exams; they might be disappointed at their own appearance; they might feel unable to make lovers or friends; they might feel as if they did not succeed at getting into the company that they wanted; and so on. One reason they do not succumb to the temptation of suicide is because they feel that these so-called failures are the fault of other people.

However, it is not necessarily the case that withdrawn children engaging in the violent behavior *completely* believe that it is their parents' fault they ended up in their current situation. Most hikikomori adolescents who engage in domestic violence have admitted to me at some point in their treatment, "I am a terrible person; I've been a continual nuisance to my parents." This is an expression of their true feelings. They are torn between self-reproach and reproaching others, and they spend their days vacillating and unable to find any psychological peace. As the psychiatrist Kandabashi Jōji has pointed out, the emotion that lies behind violence in the home is not hatred but sadness.

The Key for Dealing with Early-Stage Violence Is Not to Stimulate

The key to calm violent outbursts in the home when the child is still in the early stages is first of all not to stimulate the anger. This sounds simple, but it is unexpectedly difficult to do. To succeed at this, it is important to develop an accurate understanding of what sorts of things are likely to stimulate the child. How did it come about that he or she feels a sadness so deep that he or she feels that the only option is to lash out violently? What kinds of things should the family be paying attention to so that their child will not feel inferior and embarrassed? To find out the answers to those questions, it is necessary for the family to begin by trying to understand the nature of the child's conflict from a sympathetic point of view. It is sometimes the case that if the violent outbursts are at the very beginning stages, the violence will dissipate simply through understanding and communication.

Interventions by Others

What about more severe cases in which violent behavior has extended over a longer period of time? Needless to say, it is significantly more difficult to treat such cases. The reason is that when trying to treat cases that involve persistent outbursts of violent behavior, simply changing from one superficial tactic to another usually does not make any impact at all. There is an even more fundamental problem than that. Parents recoil, rather like a frog being stared down by a snake, and find themselves pinned down, unable to move. What solutions are there for situations that have grown that bad?

One approach that seems appropriate for such situations is to get another person involved. Of course, this does not mean asking someone else to take the violence on one's behalf. This simply means having someone else come into the household. I know of one case in which a son who was behaving terribly violently toward his mother suddenly stopped when his sister's fiancé came to live in the same home. Of course, the person in withdrawal will hate someone else coming into the middle of things, but once the change takes place, it can help calm the outbursts of violent behavior.

Getting another person involved could potentially mean calling the police. If the child is behaving in ways that are extremely violent, then the parents should of course report it to the authorities. The reason is not, however, to have the police "do something." It often happens that when the family reports the violent behavior and the police hasten to the scene, the violent tendencies go away completely. As most readers are probably aware, if a crime has not taken place, the police will probably not do much more than give the upset person a good talking to, but that is just fine. The important thing for the child to understand is "my family is prepared to call the police if need be." It might also be meaningful for the family to make a contact with a security company and make it known that if some violent behavior occurs, they will not hesitate to call a security guard. Many families might hesitate to take such measures, thinking that if they do, the retribution that would come later would be even more terrifying, but the family must not take this attitude. The family should be steadfast in reporting problems if they are severe enough to be reported, and the family must do so over and over again if necessary. If the family has the strength of their resolutions, then there is relatively little fear of retribution.

Another technique I often use to reject violence is to have the family take refuge elsewhere. What I mean is that rather than attempt to deal with the violent outburst head-on, the family should remove themselves from the scene as a way to reject it. Of course, this places a significant burden on the family, but if handled appropriately, they can expect results. Before I talk about concrete measures to do this, I would like to make one thing clear. This technique can be very effective, but it also involves a good deal of risk. If one makes an error in timing, then there is a significant chance that it will fail; therefore, before trying to use "taking refuge" as a means of therapy, it is necessary to get the help of a specialist.

"Taking Refuge": One Family's Situation

In this section, I explain how one should go about taking refuge, using the case of one family as an example. This story that I am about to tell is fiction, but only insofar as it is a composite. All of the details come from cases of real patients and families I have worked with.

The person in withdrawal was the family's firstborn son, and he had been engaging in violent outbursts in the home for over ten years. Needless to say, he did not come to the clinic for treatment himself. The sole targets of his outbursts were his mother and his brother, who was five years younger. Any trifling thing that made him unhappy would set off his anger. Any number of small incidents could trigger him—his mother might start preparing the meal too late, his brother might refuse to play a video game with him, someone might fail to change the towels in the bathroom, or the family might laugh when he was not present. Those would be enough to send him into a violent rage. The wall of his room was full of holes, and there was hardly a piece of furniture that had not been damaged. What is worse, his mother experienced a series of bruises and open wounds that hardly had a chance to heal before the next ones would come along; however, each time after he flew into one of his terrible rages, he would burst into tears and beg his mother for forgiveness. He would promise he would not harm her and would never do such a thing again. His mother told me, "I saw him behaving like that, and I couldn't help feeling sorry for him. I wanted to stay by him and help him out somehow." It is not unusual for mothers to be this self-sacrificing, but it is necessary to emphasize once again that as I mentioned earlier in this book, these kinds of relationships are codependent.

The oldest son led a rather irregular life and during the time that he was awake, he would have his mother by his side doing things for him practically the entire time. As a result, the mother could hardly go outside as she liked, and she found herself having to wait on her oldest son day and night. The son had a chronic case of insomnia, so there was never a time the family could escape the tension. The father, who was a businessman, once tried to intervene to stop the violence, but the son launched a terrible counteroffensive against him. After that, the father retreated to work where he succeeded in almost completely avoiding the situation. As the therapist working with the family, I recommended several times that the mother remove herself from the home, but the mother was concerned about the second son and found herself unable to tear herself away.

When the second son went away to college, he decided to live on his own. With him out of the house, the mother finally began to feel more like following my advice and taking refuge from the home. Right away, I decided to meet with both parents and construct a plan for them. I was worried that the father would not be supportive, but when I explained the reasons I wanted them to leave, they happily agreed to cooperate.

The oldest son's violence was almost a daily occurrence, but it came in waves, some of which were worse than others. He might do nothing but pinch or jab at them for a few days, but then he would suddenly turn increasingly violent—trying to strangle his mother, kicking her hard in the back, and doing other terrible things. Timing is all-important in taking refuge outside the home, so we decided to watch carefully for exactly the right moment.

One day, there was a big explosion. Every Sunday since the younger brother had moved away, the mother had been visiting his apartment to help him out with his laundry and cooking. That day, she had come home later than usual. The oldest son appeared to be upset by this. When she came home, he began tussling with her and struck her hard on the head. In fact, he hit her so hard that for a moment, things went black before her eyes, and she collapsed on the spot.

When the son saw his mother on the floor, he began to go into a panic. Since it was Sunday, his father was at home. He called his father and shouted, "Call an ambulance right away! Tell them her son hit her!" The father did just as he was told and called an ambulance. The son insisted that he would go, too, but the father asked him to stay at home while he took her to a nearby emergency room. While he was waiting for the results of his wife's examination, the father contacted me, and I gave him the following instructions.

"Even if she is not in bad shape, please ask the doctors to have her admitted into the hospital. If they will not admit her, please find another place to spend tonight at least. Call your oldest son as soon as you can and tell him that she is going to be in the hospital for a while. And please try not to lecture your son about his behavior."

Fortunately, the mother suffered only a mild concussion and some bleeding beneath the skin, and it was decided that she would not have to be admitted to the hospital. The father took a room at a nearby hotel and called the son from there. The son seemed to be terribly shaken up. Here is how the conversation went.

> SON: "If Mom dies or has some lasting handicap, I'm going to turn myself in and go to jail!"

> FATHER: "Your mother isn't in that bad shape, but she's going to have to spend a little while in the hospital. It seems they've got to run a bunch of tests on her."

> SON: "Then I'll go take care of her. Tell me which hospital she's in!"

FATHER: "I told the doctor you were the one who hit her. He said it's best not to let you see her for a while, so I can't tell you which hospital she's in."

The son pleaded with his father to give him the name of the hospital, swearing that he would never do such a thing again, but the father stubbornly refused, just as I had told him.

The next day, the mother called. It seemed that the son had not slept a wink the previous night.

SON: "Mom, I'm sorry. Does it still hurt? When can you come home?"

MOTHER: "The injury doesn't seem all that bad, but they're still running tests so it looks like I won't be able to come home for a little while. You make do with your father without me for the time being."

SON: "I see. I'm really sorry. Do you hate me? Will you refuse to see me?"

MOTHER: "Of course not. But the doctor ordered me not to see you for a while so instead, I'll just telephone you every day."

The son continued to beg for his mother's forgiveness and pleaded to be able to see her, thus keeping her from hanging up. In the end, the mother found she had no other choice but to put down the receiver while he was still talking. She was following the instructions I had given her earlier—I had told her to make regular calls but to be sure to hang up within five minutes every time.

Eventually, it was decided that the mother would go to stay with the younger son for a little while. The father returned home after the hospital incident, starting a life with just him and the older son alone in the house. When it was just the two of them, the son began doing the housework with surprisingly little attitude or resistance, and the violent outbursts disappeared entirely. The mother called about every other day, and the son seemed to await her call with great anticipation.

After this had continued for about two weeks, I met with the parents again. So far, things had unfolded almost completely as I had predicted, so I gave them the following instructions: "It would seem unnatural if the hospital were not to release her before long, but you cannot return home just yet. If you return now, you can rest assured that the violence will start up again. The next time you call him, this is what you should tell him.

"'The tests showed me that there was nothing terribly wrong with me, so I have been released from the hospital. But while I was in the hospital, I started thinking about a lot of things. I consulted with a therapist. Your mother is fed up with all of this violence. I've decided I'm not coming home until you really give up this violent behavior for good. Your father agrees with me that this is the right thing to do.'

"Your son will no doubt get angry, but remember that you are not 'consulting' with him; you are telling him how things are going to be. No matter how much he cries and fusses, you cannot give in to him. If you give in to him now, all of your efforts so far will be wasted."

The mother agreed and during her next telephone call, she told her son what I had instructed her to say. At first he pleaded with her over and over again, saying things like "I promise, I promise I'll never get mad with you ever again. I just want you to come home." Even so, she did not waiver in her resolve. When the son saw that, he began to get angry.

> SON: "Are you trying to abandon me? Are you trying to escape your responsibility for having raised me this way? You only love my little brother. You're a coward. I never want you to come home again!"

> MOTHER: "I took care of you for over ten years while you were beating me up, so I've more than got whatever might have been coming to me. Now we're even, fair and square. I'm not going to be coming home for a while, but that is also my house, too, so I'll return when I feel like it, and I'll call when I feel like it."

The son became furious and told her never to come home or call again, but the mother did not engage with him and simply hung up.

After that, the mother continued to make periodic calls home. At first the eldest son refused her calls, but after several days, he began to speak to her again. His conversation was the same as before—he either pleaded with her to come home or would become angry and tell her she should never come home again. In the past, whenever his mother had dealt with him, she would shrug her shoulders and give in, but this time, she responded to him in just the right way. She called him without fail at regular intervals and responded coolly and calmly to her son's entreaties. The important point here is to do this over and over again in a devoted way.

It was about two months after the mother took refuge elsewhere that the eldest son gradually began to calm down. He started yelling a lot less, and instead, he began showing a lot more sarcasm and irritation in his voice. He no longer asked her to come home but instead started saying things like "Must be nice to run away and not have a care in the world" or "It's your house, if you want to come home, do whatever you feel like." The time had come to start changing the approach. I recommended to the mother that she began watching for a time when she might made a quick, trial visit back to the house.

The mother was quite fearful and hesitant at first. Her unwillingness to go back home only made sense. After getting a taste of a peaceful life without violence for the first time in a decade, she felt all the more uneasy and frightened about the prospect of returning to her previous life; however, returning to a peaceful state was the final goal of curing her son and finding salvation for herself. I had to explain this to the mother in quite a firm way, but eventually I got her to agree.

One day, a little more than two months after she had left the home, the mother called her son like usual and casually said to him, "There's something I have to do, so I'm going to stop by the house tomorrow." The son seemed surprised and at first simply responded, "I see." In the process of talking a little more, however, he seemed to get increasingly irritated and began saying things like "So now you're finally coming home after running away. Even if you come back, there's no way I'm letting you in. Just be prepared!" The mother just answered calmly, "Don't say that. Let's have a nice meal together. It'll be the first time in ages." In the end, she left it at that.

The next day, the mother steeled her resolve and went home, but the son had stepped out of the house and was not there. The son could not shut her out of her own home, and so perhaps it was too upsetting to stay there and run the risk of meeting her face-to-face. The mother waited for him for a little while, but when he had not come home by evening, she gave up and went back to where she was staying. After repeating this a few times, the son eventually seemed to have changed his mind and indicated he would stay in to see her. The sign came when he said over the phone, "I'm sick of the food Dad makes, so come over every once in a while to make dinner, OK?"

That day was the first time in three months that the mother had come face-to-face with her son. He acted embarrassed, but without saying anything negative or hateful, he took the dinner his mother had laid out and carried it back to his room. This started a series of frequent visits by the mother back home to the house. Eventually, she accepted my suggestion to try spending a few nights back at home. Occasionally the son would say things that betrayed hints of irritation such as "People who run away don't have to worry about anything. How nice. Terrible people like me don't even have any place to run to." Nonetheless, he never engaged in violence against his mother again.

The Fundamentals of Quelling Violence

In that case, it took approximately five months for the mother to make a complete return to the family home. That was a year ago, and to date, there have not been any recurrences of violent behavior. There were times when he tried to order her around, but the relationship grew extremely stable in that there was no more violence toward the mother. Another point worthy of special note is that the relationship between the son and father had dramatically improved. There is a good, amicable relationship between the two now. Whereas the two had hardly spoken before, they often go out together for drives in the car. One might expect that once the son bottled up his violence, he would feel even more stress, but quite the contrary. If anything, he showed signs of greater activity—his appetite increased, he started going out more often, and so on. It is fair to say that forgoing violence by refusing to take part in it had extremely significant effects.

As I mentioned before, this case contains some fictional elements, but all of the details are based on real cases. In fact, this was not even my most successful case. All in all, I have had family members leave the house to escape domestic abuse in ten cases, and in all cases, this was successful in quelling the violence. What I am trying to say is that if one follows the key principles I laid out above and responds appropriately, it is not all that difficult to quell violent behavior. Those principles can lead to definite dramatic improvement, if not improve the withdrawal. If anything in the story I have just shared was idealized, it was probably the parents' reactions to my instructions. Unfortunately, it is rare that parents are quick to understand the therapist's instructions and put them into practice. It is extremely difficult to improve one's set way of doing things, especially after one has been using them for many years; however, if the parents act appropriately, then the child in withdrawal should improve significantly, as I have described here.

Once again, I would like to go over the key points of taking refuge outside the home.

- The therapist and the parents must consult extensively about the principles and methods of leaving the home.

- The immediate trigger for leaving the home should be a big burst of violence. (It is not always necessary to use hospitalization as an excuse.)

- The parent should always be sure to leave the house on the same day the violence took place.

- The parents should be sure to call the child that very same day.

- The parent who left should tell the child "I will contact you regularly. You do not need to worry about your livelihood. I will return home sometimes, but I'm not exactly sure when that will be. I can't tell you where I'm staying. I won't return until the violence is completely gone."

- The parent should tell the child that he or she decided on this course of action in consultation with a doctor in the hopes of curing the child, and the entire family agreed with this course of action.

- The parent should call periodically after that, but should be sure only to speak five minutes each time. When the time comes, the parent should hang up, even if it is in the middle of the conversation.

- The parent should watch his or her timing, trying to find a moment when the child has settled down, then he or she can begin returning home or spending the night at home, but only on a temporary basis.

- When the parent spends the night at home, if there is no violence, and if the child is able to speak calmly, then it is possible to return home.

- The parents should stay in close touch with a therapist through all of this.

- The parents should not give in to violence or threats. They should stay steadfast and honest.

- Each case requires a different amount of time before the parents can return home for good. If the child is in a less severe case of withdrawal, the parents might return in a month, but in more severe cases, it often takes half a year for the parent to return.

Considering that this is a book about hikikomori cases, some might feel that I have placed too much emphasis on dealing with domestic violence. Of course, I have reasons for doing so. As I explained before, it is not all that difficult to quell violent behavior in the household, but even so, almost half of all families are forced to deal with their child's violent behavior before they can even start dealing with the withdrawal. I have provided concrete instructions for dealing with violent behavior within as short a time frame as possible so that parents can get to the heart of the matter as quickly as possible. One can only start dealing with the withdrawal head-on once the violence has been quelled.

11 | TREATMENT AND RETURNING TO SOCIETY

When Treatment Begins Late

Some patients do not improve at the rate one would hope for, even when all measures have been handled appropriately. Also, there are limits as to how much a family can do to help their child return to society when they are working alone. For that reason, it is essential that the family consults a therapeutic facility with specialists, even if that means that the family goes first, without bringing their child with them. When I say "therapeutic facility," I mean facilities that have psychiatric doctors. I do not have enough experience with other kinds of facilities to be able to say much about them; however, I can say that my enthusiasm for outpatient counseling by psychologists and doctors of psychosomatic medicine is somewhat more reserved—it is *possible* that such kinds of treatment could be effective. There are some kinds of treatment facilities and treatments, however, that are harmful and should be avoided: private facilities that institutionalize the patients but do not provide treatment by a medical doctor, hypnotists, self-help seminars, new religions, and other civil nonmedical organizations.

In the chapter about the hikikomori system, I mentioned that it is all too common for families to start therapy too late when dealing with social withdrawal. Our survey showed that although the average age for the onset of withdrawal was 15.5 years old, the average age at which the patients started receiving treatment was 19.6. In other words, 4.1 years elapses between the average ages for the onset of the withdrawal and the first visit to a therapist. Also, only 2.5 percent of the respondents had officially lost their position at school or work by the time that their withdrawal began, but 45 percent had lost their position by the time they started receiving therapy. Why does it take so long for so many people to get into therapy?

The foremost reason is that it is difficult to link the feelings of apathy and the withdrawal to a specific diagnosis. Hikikomori patients do not demonstrate the same clear signs of abnormality as a schizophrenic, and the conflicts that they experience are right on the borderline separating normal experience from the pathological, so typically, they do not express a strong desire on their own part to undergo treatment. Because of this, people think they are being "lazy" when they are beginning to slip into withdrawal. In fact, it is not just ordinary people who say such things. It is not unheard-of for psychiatrists to say "they don't have a psychological illness so just leave them alone" or "they're just being lazy, so maybe you should give them some physical work or something to do."

As if that were not a big enough problem, it is exceedingly rare to be able to get the person in withdrawal to come to the treatment facility when the family first seeks counseling. Because of this, it is important that the family is willing to come alone for regular consultations while they wait for their child to show signs of wanting to undergo treatment. Unfortunately, under the current system of insurance, even though it is necessary for the family to have insurance when starting therapy, it is difficult for the parents to keep coming for consultations if they are coming by themselves. Moreover, it is also not uncommon for families to be shooed away at the gate of clinical facilities that say, "We can't help you unless the person with the problem comes here himself." Directly or indirectly, these factors make it difficult for families to start coming to a psychiatric clinic. Therefore, the first thing that the family must do is find a local clinic that has a great deal of experience dealing with the adolescent problems and that will make it easy for the parents to seek consultation, even if their child is not present.

How to Choose a Psychiatric Clinic

There are several key points to keep in mind when choosing a psychiatric clinic. People often say that the university hospitals have the most reliable clinical facilities, but that is not always true. In fact, I think it is safe to say that at the present moment, university hospitals are not the best choice when it comes to treating cases of people in withdrawal.

We have an impression that university hospitals are the places where talented young medical doctors gather, working with famous professors and associate professors. That image is not necessarily incorrect; however, we must not forget that universities are designed to carry out research and education. People tend to believe high-quality facilities that provide specialty treatments are best found at university hospitals, so as a result, university hospitals are often extremely crowded. As patients come surging in, there is a tendency for the doctor to end up inadvertently simplifying the therapy sessions or treating the patient in a perfunctory manner. It is often the case that students and interns are present as observers during the therapy sessions. In the case of adolescents in particular, it is easy for this to become a burden. Of course, it is possible for the patients or their families to say that they do not want any outside observers present during the consultation, but most people do not seem to do that.

That being said, the level of specialization that one finds in a university setting can be useful. Most places have good facilities for examining new patients and well-established arrangements for referring patients to other clinics, so university hospitals can be good for the first stage of consultation. It is not a bad idea to consult first with a university hospital if one suspects that the patient is not merely experiencing a simple, straightforward case of withdrawal.

What should one do when searching for a regular psychiatric clinic that is not in a university setting? The fastest thing to do is to consult with a local public health department. The situation differs a great deal from one public health department to another, but there is an increasing number that are concerned about hikikomori cases, so it is possible that they might be able to provide a referral to a place that would be well suited to deal with the issue.

There are ways to look for places in books and catalogs. Libraries and bookstores are full of books about psychological issues. Among them, one can find guidebooks to counseling facilities. The ones that I find most valuable are the resources published by the National

Alliance for the Families of the Mentally Ill (Zenkoku Seishin Shōgaisha Kazoku-kai Rengō-kai).[1] (See the bibliography at the end of this book.) Its publications provide a rather comprehensive introduction to all of the reputable psychiatric clinics and counseling facilities throughout the country. If one looks for a facility using this resource, one should probably select a handful of institutions within commuting distance, and then give each a telephone call. At that time, one should find out the answers to two important questions: "Do you deal with patients who are adolescents?" and "For the time being, it is not possible for our son (or daughter) to come in, so would it be all right if we as parents came in for a consultation on our own?"

Personally, I recommend newly established psychiatric offices and clinics run by individual doctors. These days, there are many young psychiatrists who are setting up their own offices. Many are willing to treat adolescent problems, and often they are among the most eager to use new treatments in their practice. It is fair to expect that they will build good clinical relationships with the patient and family, both in terms of technique and service.

Getting the Hikikomori into Treatment

Once there has been a decision about which clinic to use, the parents should start regular sessions on their own, trying to understand how to best deal with their child and improve the environment at home. At the same time, the parents should start gradually urging their withdrawn child to start coming with them to the clinic.

First, parents should find the right moment to tell their child they have been going regularly to receive counseling. They should break it to the child directly, without beating around the bush. For instance, they might say, "We are worried about you, so we've starting going for counseling. The doctor says he'd like to meet with you, too." Usually, the child will refuse to be seen by a doctor at first, so one should not pursue the issue too tenaciously just yet. There are some instances in which the child will insist it is "not necessary" for them to go the hospital, even if they are going alone, but if the parent explains, "we are worried, so we want to go for counseling—just the two of us parents," then the child will usually relent and accept it.

After that, every time the parents go to the clinic, they should talk to the child and invite him or her along. It is best not to pressure the child about going until the day of the appointment; instead, they should invite the child to go that morning. It is often the case with hikikomori patients that their moods change with the day. Moreover, inviting them to go too far in advance can place subtle pressures on them. It is not unusual for people in withdrawal to agree to go see the doctor, but when the day of the appointment actually rolls around, they start saying they do not want to go. If this is repeated multiple times, both the child and the family gradually begin to lose hope, and the idea of going to the clinic begins to seem like an insurmountable barrier. To prevent this, it is best to extend the invitation on the morning of the day of the appointment. If the child does not want to go, then the parents should not push him or her; they should just go by themselves to receive counseling, and then when they come home, they should talk about what the doctor said and mention the date of the next appointment. It is also a good idea to put the next appointment on the calendar.

In the process of repeating these subtle forms of urging, the child will gradually begin to show interest. Sometimes, the child will ask, "What did the doctor have to say today?" or other similar questions. If the family makes it this far, then it is just a matter of time before the child comes around and consents to go along.

What Is Important Is a Relationship of Trust with the Doctor

What sorts of treatment will the doctor use at the clinic? Let me say a few words about that here, but before that, I should mention that there is no specific, special "treatment" for social withdrawal. It is not necessary to check the patient into a special institution or give him or her a specialized psychiatric treatment. At the same time, it is not a condition that will simply go away if the patient begins taking medicine. While I am on the subject of medication, I should mention briefly there is not any medicine that can effectively cure social withdrawal. There is the antidepressant Prozac, which has become a best seller in the United States in recent years. Prozac has dramatically few side effects and is easy to use, so it has become extremely well known for allowing patients to be proactive and change their way of life. This drug is being imported and prescribed in Japan with increasing frequency. I have had a number of patients who have tried Prozac, but it has been so ineffective at treating social withdrawal that I think it is safe to say that it has no effect whatsoever. My impression is that, if anything, it tends to bring out undesirable tendencies in patients—they seem to become aggressive or violent. Of course, the evaluation of the effectiveness of a drug is something that should done carefully over time, but I do not expect effective results in curing withdrawal. In reality, however, most hikikomori patients who are receiving treatment are prescribed at least a small amount of antidepressants or antianxiety drugs to help them cope with their symptoms.

In treating a hikikomori patient, the most important thing is for the patient to develop a relationship of deep trust with the doctor. In the survey of psychiatrists that I introduced previously, many respondents answered that "sharing a forum with a doctor" was meaningful in treating patients. It is necessary for the psychiatrist to be sympathetic, form an established relationship of trust, and maintain a "shared forum" with the patient that will continue over a long period of time. In dealing with social withdrawal, the most important techniques to achieve these goals are, just as one might expect, the basic techniques of psychiatry. In my own clinical experiences, I cannot recall requiring special techniques other than the ones described in this book.

The doctor must also be in a position of patience—one that allows him or her to wait. In other words, it is important that the doctor be willing to wait for change without growing impatient. There is an expression "the medicine of time," which means that time is one of the most important elements in healing. In the end, I believe that there is no better way of going about treatment than taking one's time and continuing with the tried-and-true techniques.

"Routes" to Return to Society

When the treatment is going well, the household has grown less tense, and a deeper level of communication has been established in the family, then it is time to proceed with a more active form of treatment. What is most important in the next stage is to encourage relations outside the family while promoting further maturation of the patient. In a sense, once the situation inside the family has grown stable, one should help the patient gradually begin turning outward.

If patients are in the first stages of social withdrawal or seem to have relatively few problems dealing with people outside the family, they can sometimes return to society relatively quickly by themselves, provided that their families handle them in appropriate ways. From this stage forward, the patient's progress may vary widely, depending on how able they are to form relationships with others. The ability to interact with other people can be earned only through actually interacting with others. How can one encourage a hikikomori son or daughter to go out and meet others in person, thus gaining more experience interacting with others? That can sometimes be extremely difficult.

Any number of ways could help a person return to society, if one only looks for them. There are places that patients can go and practical things that patients can do that would not place too much psychological strain on them. They might take easy part-time jobs, go do things at a culture center, take classes in computers or word processing, take classes at private English-language schools, participate in cooking workshops, do volunteer activities, study at a driving school, and so on. Parents should consult with their child to consider what kinds of places or activities might be best for him or her.

If the patient has an unusually difficult time interacting with people, this stage can involve some of the most difficult barriers to progress. Things might be stable in the household, but the patient might simply be unable to set foot outside. Unable to take advantage of the various chances waiting outside, he or she might lose confidence and slip into an even deeper state of withdrawal. Even the relatively approachable kinds of activities that I mentioned before might seem too overwhelming. In the past, I have sometimes introduced patients to day-care facilities designed specifically for psychological patients and provided by the local public health department or psychological health centers. Such day-care facilities provide various practical activities and work projects that can be valuable in helping the patient.

It is unfortunate, however, that many people in withdrawal refuse to go these facilities because of pride. If one can help them get over that and start going, one can expect positive results, so it is not a bad idea to keep such facilities in mind as a possible route to return to society.

When one is thinking about possible routes to help the patient return to society, one important factor to consider is the self-motivation of the patient. If anything, it is rare for adolescents in withdrawal to return to society without a hitch, following the rails that people around them have laid. It is sometimes the case that patients will refuse all of the suggestions provided by their parents but then, much to everyone's surprise, come up with a solution on their own. In fact, cases like this are the most likely to go well. One case that left a particular impression on me involved a patient who was in withdrawal for several months but then started going on daily outings to a local fishing spot. There was a small, informal group of people who also fished there, and before long, they got to be on quite friendly terms with him. I had not expected the patient to seek out these encounters, so the new friendships were an unexpected surprise. In fact, there is nothing better than routes that the patient discovers by himself or herself; however, such discoveries are possible only in mild cases of withdrawal—cases in which the patient has a sincere desire to get better.

Trying Meaningful "Hangouts"

A few moments ago, I wrote briefly about day-care facilities; however, for people in withdrawal, their biggest problem is in their inability to interact with outsiders. They are completely normal in terms of the ability to perform the various tasks necessary in daily life. Choosing a course of action designed for a person with a mental illness can cause various problems for the person in withdrawal, so it is difficult to generalize about that as a course of action. What is necessary for the hikikomori is a facility or some other "route" that provides a site for healing—a place where the person coming out of withdrawal can learn techniques and gain experience interacting with other people.

I am a member of a "youth health center," which provides a club that helps young people interact with their peers—a kind of "hangout" that members pay a small fee to belong to. I have served as a staff member and collaborator with this club for some years, and over time I have sent them dozens of my hikikomori patients.

This club has activities only twice a week for two hours at a time, but sometimes the results can be dramatic. At my urging, one of my patients who had experienced difficulty and fear with interacting with others began participating in the club. He made his first-ever close friend there; he gained experience in talking with girls, and he found his confidence restored—something that would have impossible if he had been left on his own. Such experiences can be invaluable for the withdrawn patient. Of course, it sometimes takes many years before people in withdrawal begin to feel as if they want to try participating in a club like the one I have just described. It is also the case that some patients might start attending a club but do not find themselves fitting in; if so, they might drop out altogether. If the conditions are right, however, and patients are able to participate in such clubs, then they will often be more effective than other options such as hospitalization, which I discuss more below.

One patient of mine, a person who was in a severe state of withdrawal, suddenly started going to the club after two years of me recommending that he go. There he made several close friends, and he became much more able to lead an interactive life. After trying a number of different part-time jobs, he is currently back in high school part-time. In addition, I had another patient who starting doing volunteer activities while using the club. Another used the club as a stepping-stone to take a part-time job—a good job that treats its workers like full-time employees. He has held this job for some time now. In short, this club has produced a number of success stories.

For a "hangout" like this to be effective, I believe it needs to meet the following criteria.

- There should be a number of specialists on staff who are actively engaged in coordinating the meetings and encouraging interactions between members.

- It should not be a place where "anything goes." The staff should, to a certain extent, establish a list of possible activities. (At the very least, the members should not be the main ones in charge. The reason is that this makes it easier for everyone to participate, and it prevents members from restricting the autonomy of other members.)

• The goal right off the bat should not be to "invigorate" or "improve the abilities" of the members. The purpose should be to foster intimacy between participants.

• The members should be more or less restricted to people in a state of social withdrawal. To phrase it in a different way, the organizers should carefully consider whether or not to accept other kinds of patients, including delinquents, borderline cases, or people who have a tendency to act out.

• The organizers should make members feel that their psychological well-being is being protected. To do so, organizers should provide punitive rules that restrict the participation or even ban members who exhibit frequent problematic behavior.

• People interested in participating should always have a letter of introduction from the doctor in charge of their case, and there should be a committee to screen letters of introduction. (In other words, it should be a condition that members should be undergoing medical treatment at the same time that they participate.)

• The space of the club should just serve as a springboard, and the group should respect the expansion of relations and activities outside the group.

• As an option, the group could consider providing subgroups with more specific purposes, such as study groups or clubs within the club.

• It should have a forum for guardians to participate, too; for instance, it might provide a place for parents to interact with each other in a family association or some similar kind of group.

• Rather than just do things within the space of the club itself, it should actively encourage activities that engage the outside world, such as going to see movies or bowling together.

• To keep the group going, it is unavoidable that there should be a fee for membership, but the amount should not be high enough that it prevents people from participating.

These guidelines were put together by the person in charge of the club that I mentioned before, a gentleman whom I respect highly. In rewriting them here, there are a few spots that I tweaked to reflect my own hopes for the group. Perhaps I even idealized the guidelines a little, but it is no exaggeration to say that all of these rules are ones we currently put into practice. It would be much easier to fight the hikikomori problem if there were organizations like this everywhere, taking this club's activities as a model.

The Possibilities of Computer and Internet Communication

Recent years have seen continual progress in technology, especially in personal computing. New technology is constantly being invented, but what is most relevant here is how easy it has become to engage in different kinds of communication. The new form of communication known as e-mail has made it radically easier to expand one's breadth of contacts and exchanges. I believe that it can be useful, in its own way, for people in a state of social withdrawal to use computers.

Right now, I am using online communication and the Internet to keep in contact with some of my patients: however, I am not using it for counseling; I am using it as a forum for basic kinds of ordinary chit-chat. I am also experimenting with using online tools to create a network between multiple patients and encourage communication. If we use this network, the same message will be distributed to all of the members; therefore, it is possible to exchange opinions simultaneously between multiple people. It has been two years since I started using this network. Since then, it has been a stepping-stone for several members. One became interested in computers and started studying programming languages; other members started participating in other mailing lists (which are like larger versions of the "network" that I mentioned a moment ago). Some members are even starting to participate in offline, face-to-face meetings with one another.

I believe that the personal computer can be extremely significant as a tool, especially in the lives of people in social withdrawal. This is not just limited to communications and the use of the Internet. A variety of possibilities open up when one learns to use a computer. It is probably helpful in gaining employment, but that is not what I am talking about. Through the computer, it is possible to share conversations with others, and the impact of this can be enormous. Having a computer can be especially significant once communication has been restored within the family. If hikikomori are better with the computer than the members of their family, then it becomes possible for them to teach their parents. For patients who quietly yearn to be useful to their families, the ability to put their technological know-how to work and teach their parents a thing or two can seem like a perfect opportunity. Also, if they become good at using e-mail, they can stay in frequent contact with family members, for instance, if the father is temporarily living away from the family for work. It can sometimes even be useful even when people are living under the same roof, in that e-mail can allow someone to express what is on his or her mind without verbalizing it directly.

One often hears concerns that people in withdrawal will get worse if they spend all of their time with the computer; however, as I just mentioned, the computer can help *enrich* relationships with other people. Even when it does not, it usually does not aggravate the state of withdrawal. It may look from the outside as if the person in withdrawal were running away from life by spending lots of time with the computer, but if he or she is using it to connect with other people, then it is performing a role in helping him or her establish a point of contact with society.

Treatment in a Hospital, Specialized Housing, Etc.

When a patient is not making any progress with outpatient treatment, it can be effective to check him or her into a hospital and provide treatment there, but that is effective only in cases where the patient wants it to happen. In general, however, I cannot heartily recommend "mental hospitals." The main purpose of trying to give a patient treatment in the hospital is ostensibly to help him or her get experience in dealing with the outside world, but treatment does not necessarily mean much in hospital wards where most patients are people with serious mental illness. If necessary, the best kind of environment would be a relatively open one with relatively young patients. Environments that would allow the patient to interact with members of the opposite sex are especially desirable.

The kind of "lodging treatment" advocated by Dr. Inamura is not used very often these days, but it can be extremely helpful in treating cases of social withdrawal. What I am referring to is a kind of communal living in which a handful of staff members live with approximately ten or so lodgers. Through various activities and daily life guidance from the staff, this kind of environment can help improve the condition of patients in withdrawal. Close communal living with people of the same age group can sometimes bring about unexpected changes in the condition of patients who have an especially difficult time interacting with other people. There has not yet been enough formulation of this kind of treatment, but I expect that this kind of treatment will begin to show results rather like the ones I described above in the section about hangouts.

Let me say a word or two about the idea of groups for the families of patients. Parents who are dealing with hikikomori children are fighting a continual, lonely battle, day in and day out. Sometimes this loneliness can lead parents to feel frustrated, as if they were entirely on their own in the world. This sense just strengthens the vicious circle of what I have called the hikikomori system. I believe it is desirable for the families of people in withdrawal to come together and form connections with one another, much like the families of people who are dealing with other kinds of mental illness. The reason is that when families with similar problems form connections, it helps them maintain psychological stability during their long battles. The problem here, however, is that the creation of such groups lags behind the development of the hikikomori issue itself. Presently, there are far too few groups for the families of people in withdrawal, and what do exist are too small-scale. Currently, I am in charge of a course that meets once a month and is called "Hands-On Work with Withdrawal." The families of about fifty people come each time. I hope that this group will gradually come to function as a support organization for families of people facing similar problems.

The Milestone of Age Thirty

Sometimes I have had families who are in the following situation come to consult with me. Treatment has gone well, and the patient has reached what I call the final stages, but they are unable to go any farther. The patient is going to treatment, and there is smooth conversation within the family, but the family does not know what to do beyond that.

First, I should say that cases like that are really exceptional. As far as I know, I believe one could say that if the treatment has progressed sufficiently so that the patient is in the last stages yet does not emerge from a state of withdrawal, then there is probably a problem somewhere in the routes of communication. Rather than lament a lack of progress, it is probably necessary to consult with a specialist to see if there is indeed enough communication. But what if it does turn out that there does not seem to be a problem? What can one do about cases that simply do not seem to get better? I take up that question in this section.

If the withdrawn state has continued for over a decade, or if the patient age is already approaching the age of forty, I think it is necessary to look at the situation stoically and begin thinking about the following steps. Unfortunately, there will probably be more and more cases like this in the future. When the parents reach retirement age or become ill, it becomes difficult, if not impossible, to continue working toward treatment in the same untiring way as before. In those situations, and especially when financial hardship is involved, I believe that the family should undertake a realistic reassessment of their situation.

When a hikikomori son or daughter reaches the age of thirty, the family should treat that as an important milestone. To be more concrete, the families should have a discussion with him or her about the long-term future. This discussion might turn quite serious in nature. Of course, I doubt anyone would think that it would be better to let this "milestone" go by without paying any attention, simply waiting for the situation to get worse. I think one reason that it is often so difficult to talk about withdrawal has to do with this. Most therapists do not necessarily have the courage to lay out a specific, responsible answer about where the "milestone" age should be. It is my hope that my suggestion that thirty represents a critical age is not only helpful in practice but will also help provoke discussion among specialists.

Sharing "Prospects"

At this milestone, when the family and the hikikomori child engage in their discussions, I think that the family should raise three points: (1) the prospects for treatment, (2) financial prospects, and (3) the prospect of participating in society. In regard to the first of these issues, namely, the prospects for treatment, the family should first reconsider the methods currently being used and should emphasize that the family is not going to be able to participate in treatment forever. This is connected to the second issue, financial prospects, but the family should bring up the possibility of trying to get public assistance so that the costs of treatment are covered through taxpayer money. They should also broach the subject of having the patient designated as having a disability.

Here I have dared to use the word *disability.* Of course, I do not mean to hurt the feelings of the patient who has suffered for so long in a withdrawn state; however, I believe that if a person has been in a continual state of withdrawal for nearly a decade, then one no longer can casually assure them, "You are not sick, so don't worry about it." When the state of withdrawal continues for a long time and grows increasingly worse, then the question is no longer really one of whether or not the person is sick. If anything, the problem is, in a certain sense, much more serious than a simple illness. People in withdrawal also experience an awareness that they have a sort of handicap and feel pressure to change their lives in some way or another. If things have gone for such a long time, I cannot, as a therapist, simply close my eyes and continue to say to a patient that he or she is "fine." I believe that if doctors are really performing their role as a specialist and looking clearly at the prospects for their patients, then they have a responsibility to say such things. When I am talking about "prospects," I am specifically referring to situations in which a patient does not seem to have any hope of getting better as a result of the treatment that he or she has been undergoing for an extended period of time. There is a possibility that a "realistic" assessment, if shared by the family and the patient himself or herself, can help the patient progress to the next level.

Explaining the Family's Economic Situation

As the state of withdrawal grows increasingly prolonged, parents will likely retire and start living off their pensions. If the hikikomori state continues, then the parents may die while their child is still at home. Aging and death are hard facts for the parents, and no one can do anything to stop them. When the child in withdrawal reaches the "milestone" of age thirty, the parents should take the initiative and make a concerted effort to help their child recognize these facts. The family should not hide anything; they should convey to their child the financial outlook of the entire family. This probably involves creating a will and testament that expresses their hopes for their child and shows their concern for his or her future.

First, parents should explain the financial situation of the family in as much detail as possible, including an explanation of any assets or loans they might have. They should explain in concrete terms how that will change after they retire. In addition, they should explain what will happen in the event of the deaths of both parents. These days, it is recommended that one create a will early in life before things get too late, but another reason one should consider creating a will is because it can potentially have a positive impact on treatment. Of course, the family can expect the child to show resistance. Families that have assets might not be comfortable with the idea of letting the child know that they have some financial leeway, fearing that the child might come to the conclusion that he or she can continue on living without worrying about finances. Conversely, if a family does not have a lot of room financially, the family might worry that their child will begin to fret needlessly. These worries are entirely understandable, but in my experience, these situations do not usually come to pass.

Realistically, the thing that fans the flames of the child's anxiety most are threats without any concrete details. "Your parents will not be alive forever." "We don't any money to spare at all." Vague threats like these will only be harmful. On the other hand, a calm and honest discussion that involves realistic, concrete details is, if anything, likely to give a sense of relief—a sense that "I am trusted as a member of this family."

Among the patients I have treated, there was one young man who came out of withdrawal after many years and got a part-time job as a result of his father falling ill and the family's subsequent economic crisis. If the parents are trying to create a sense of urgency, it is best to tell their child the truth and show him or her the numbers in a realistic and concrete way. Trying to create a sense of urgency without sharing concrete numbers and details is tantamount to simple threats and intimidation. The actions might seem similar, but in reality, they are completely different.

Redrawing the Starting Line

What kinds of options exist if the parents reach retirement and start living off their pensions, but they continue to have difficulty holding a realistic discussion about the family's financial outlook? My suggestions are these. If the child is going to continue not to work, then the family should consider separating the household so that the child is legally independent, and then apply for aid from welfare. If the case involves psychological symptoms, then I might recommend that the patient receive a disability pension.

The prospect of starting to receive a disability pension can sometimes aid in the process of treatment. This is because it can help the patient properly accept the fact that he or she is currently living with a handicap. In most cases, the patient will refuse the idea of welfare or a disability pension, claiming that going to such measures is beyond the pale. Sometimes he or she will express distrust in the therapist. I believe, however, that bringing up realistic situations like this will, in the long run, actually support the recovery of the withdrawn patient. The reason I say this is that all the cases in which I have recommended that a patient begins receiving welfare, the patient ends up accepting my suggestion and eventually arriving at a more balanced psychological state.

When the discussions make it this far, the subject is, in a way, already starting to turn to the third item mentioned above, namely, the prospect of participating in society. In other words, at this stage, there is a reconsideration of routes that would allow the patient to participate in society. The patient must accept that he or she is not at all different from other psychiatric patients in that he or she is reliant on outside society. Accepting this takes a great deal of courage, but if the patient accepts this once and for all, then it becomes possible for him or her to "take the offensive," in the best sense of the phrase. At that point, the child can begin thinking about using rehabilitative facilities for psychological patients, such as workshops or day-care facilities offered by public health facilities and psychological health centers. I have seen several patients who have gone into such workshops, regained their sense of leadership little by little, thus reaching the point that they could take up some form of work.

This does not necessarily mean that the patient is "giving up." If anything, one can expect that new possibilities will open up for the patient once he or she accepts his or her limitations. It is because I have seen patients experience positive improvement that I dare to make these suggestions, which to some readers may seem quite extreme.

12 | THE SOCIAL PATHOLOGY OF WITHDRAWAL

Have Youth Really Become More Apathetic?

It was about twenty years ago that student apathy appeared on the social scene. People began to use words like "the principle of three no's" *(sanmushugi)* and "the disenchanted generation" *(shirake sedai)* to describe the increasingly apathetic attitudes of young people in Japan.[1] One could say many things about student apathy and its connection to the zeitgeist of the era.

Since then, has there been an increase in the intensity of the apathy that young people feel? I do not feel that there has been. Does that mean then that young people will always be apathetic? Or could that mean that the phenomenon of the so-called increasing apathy among today's youth is really nothing more than an illusion?

For people like me who were young during the 1970s, the so-called increasing apathy of youth seems like nothing more than a struggle of values between different generations. I suppose one could say that we did not act out or we did not burn with a strong sense of moral obligation, engaging in politics or social action. But doesn't every generation get caught up or throw its heart and soul into something that, from the viewpoint of the previous generation, looks like nothing more than a mere diversion? One cannot say that *otaku* are any more apathetic than the participants in Zenkyōtō.[2] I tend to be skeptical. I suspect that it is possible to call a generation completely apathetic only when talking in closed conversations with listeners who share the same views as the speaker—conversations among people trying to sum up an entire generation in a single breath.

I believe the rise in student apathy has something to do with the fact that in the postwar period, there has been an unprecedented rise in the number of people who continue from high school into college. If the number of students has increased, then it is only makes sense that the number of dropouts has also increased. People often talk about the "diversification or relativizing of values" to account for this, but I think that one can think of this from a completely different perspective. In an era in which everyone can go to college, people begin to share a set of values and take the idea of going to college for granted.[3] If anything, this helps create a consistency in values. Nonetheless, it is true that the act of going through one test after another, like passing through a series of barriers, does not confer any special privileges or guarantees other than giving the student a reprieve from participating in society for a limited period of time. Why *wouldn't* it be hard to go through this process without falling into a state of "apathy" along the way?

In looking at the experiences of people in withdrawal, it becomes clear that the standards for adapting to "school" and adapting to "society" are quite different. How common is it for a student to go through college without any real problems, reach graduation, then get stuck at the stage where he or she is supposed to find a job? As I mentioned before, very few of the hikikomori cases I have seen involve extensive employment experience. When one considers this relatively consistent fact in relation to the broad variety of backgrounds seen among patients in withdrawal—ranging from people who only graduated from middle school all the way to people who have graduated from elite universities—one can tell that the gap between the standard values of school and society is an extremely serious problem. This does not simply mean that what people are learning in school is not useful in society. To put it simply, the kinds of relationships one has in school and the kinds of relationships that one has in society are quite different.

In a nutshell, the difference has to do with the consciousness of one's role. When people are out working as members of society, to accept the specific role that is expected of them in the workplace, there is an obligation for them to relinquish all the other possible roles they *could* play. This act of "relinquishing then accepting" is something that students are completely unable to learn in the educational system of our country.

An Education System That Compels Students to "Disavow Castration"

Social withdrawal is a pathology of adolescence. This suggests that the problem of withdrawal is linked closely to our current educational system. No doubt, there are many different kinds of social pathology that have to do with withdrawal, but when we consider that the first "societies" children will know are their family, and then school, it becomes clear that we must think critically about how our educational system is set up.

To come right to the point, our current educational system is one that compels students to "disavow castration." What does that mean? First, let me say a few words about "castration." As my readers surely know, castration means the removal of the penis. In psychoanalysis, the concept of castration is extremely important. Why is that? Because castration has to do with the growth of all people, regardless of whether they are biologically male or female. In psychoanalysis, the penis is used as a symbol for what is almighty and can do anything. As children grow, they are forced to recognize through their interactions with other people that they are not all-powerful, almighty beings. The act of giving up on the notion that one is almighty and powerful is called "castration" by psychiatrists.

It is by realizing that one is *not* all-powerful and omnipotent that one develops the need for the first time to interact with other people. Sometimes certain people happen to be blessed with different sorts of abilities, and seem to belong to some sort of "elite," but at the same time, they might lack social qualities. This shows the importance of "castration" but in the opposite way. In other words, if people are *not* castrated in the symbolic sense, they cannot participate in the social system. It is probably safe to say that this is true for all human society, regardless of ethnicity or culture. Growth and maturation is a repeated process of loss repeated over and over again. The pain of growing up is the pain of castration, but the difficulty of castration is that it is something that must be forced on you by other people. One cannot wish on one's own to be castrated.

Now that I have explained what is meant by castration, let me pause to reflect on the nature of school. Clearly, there are two opposing aspects to school. There is the "homogenizing" aspect that places value on things like equality, majority decision making, and individuality, but there is also a "differentiating" aspect that places value on report cards and measuring how far students deviate from the mean. As members of a group, children are treated homogeneously, but once that homogeneity is asserted, students are then subjected to a process of differentiation. It is because students are differentiated in an environment where they are supposed to be treated homogeneously that school becomes a hotbed of jealousy and bullying, but that is a topic for another time. One other important point about our educational system is that the entire system delays participation in society for all of those who are in it; perhaps it even functions as a device that places a moratorium on self-determination, delaying it to a later date. School gives students shelter, but in return, it imposes its own unique set of values on them.

In school, students are forced to share the illusion that everyone has infinite possibilities. This is a problem in that children, who are already in the process of being castrated, are urged to participate in this illusion, which appears entirely tempting to them. In other words, students try to disavow their castration.

It may seem to readers that I am trying to criticize the culture of Japanese postwar democracy rather like the Japan Teachers' Union used to do.[4] Before engaging in this sort of criticism, however, we should emphasize one thing. It was we ourselves who ceaselessly sought out this kind of educational system. That is an incontrovertible fact.

Gender Differences and What They Mean

The "temptation to disavow castration" becomes an issue, for instance, when one thinks of gender and the ways it is implicated in cases of social withdrawal. I have said this before, but the overwhelming number of cases of social withdrawal involve men. In the survey I talked about before, 80 percent of the cases I have dealt with have been men. It is a commonly accepted theory that "student apathy" is also a problem that occurs only among men. Why?

As one explanation, one could point to the high expectations placed on men in modern Japanese society—expectations that are generally higher than those placed on women. There is an expectation that by the time a man grows out of his teenage years, he will be participating in society in some fashion, either through working at a job or through holding down a position in school. People are likely to criticize him if he is not. Women, however, are sometimes able to continue living at home without necessarily participating in society, especially if people say that she is just "helping out with things around the house." There is also a general expectation in Japan that when a woman marries, she will become a wife and a housekeeper. One could say that people are less likely to see a woman withdrawing into the household as problematic behavior, and the amount of stress caused by outside expectations is likely to be that much less. Recent years have seen rapid changes in the ways that Japanese society divides social responsibility based on gender lines, but even so, those divisions still remain deeply rooted even now.

Let me put this another way. In Japan the entire social system functions to "castrate" people, and women in particular, and so perhaps it is easier for women to mature at a faster rate. From an early age, women are treated as "girls," and so they are forced to be feel resigned. That is one reason young women are typically more mature than young men of the same age. Even when they are not, young men are rarely able to hold a candle to young women's ability to calculate and look at the realities of the world. As a result, the compulsion to try and disavow castration that one finds throughout the educational system does not work as well with women who are already familiar with feelings of resignation.

Accept or Reject, Both Produce the Same Results

What are the effects of the compulsion brought about by the educational system to try and disavow castration? The most troubling aspect of the system is that one gets the same results if one submits to the system or one stands in direct opposition to it. What do I mean? Regardless of whichever position one takes, in the end, one does not end up reaching full social maturity.

Let me give a different but similar scenario. A mother who tells her child to rely on her completely will end up compelling her child to try to disavow castration in order to maintain a degree of emotional independence. Reliance on the mother is the premise whether the child is accepting a position of reliance on her or is mounting a challenge to her. In other words, the temptation to "disavow castration" draws a person in, regardless of whether a person accepts or rebels. I will go out on a limb and make a bold statement that people who would ordinarily be seen as "elites" and a certain portion of students who "refuse school" share a point of commonality in their inability to adapt—a point of commonality has to do with "narrowness of values" and "self-centeredness." I am not trying to criticize these groups by writing this. These two groups act in their own ways to the best of their abilities, but in doing so, they arrive at similar results. By pointing out this tragic fact, I am expressing my doubts about the current state of the educational system today.

The majority of young people who have gone into withdrawal are continually cursing the illusion of equality forced on them during their earlier lives at school. It is not that difficult to find signs that they are resisting the disavowal of their castration. In fact, aren't young people who go into withdrawal condemned to unending adolescence, victims of the disavowal of castration that they are forced into? I cannot help but think so.

If we stop and consider things from the point of view of the hikikomori adolescent, I would have to say that at this era of ours—and by this, I do *not* mean our country—we still have not correctly understood the meaning of freedom. It is possible to see the state of withdrawal as extremely free in that the person in withdrawal is exempt from any social bonds. However, the people whom most would consider even freer are condemned to even less freedom. In this point, I sense the pathology of our era—the failure to understand and enjoy freedom to its fullest sense. In our era, "being free" itself seems to be a source of conflict. Some have said that this is an "era of adolescence"; if that is the case, then I cannot help but feel but that "social withdrawal" is the pathology that best symbolizes our moment in time.

CONCLUSION
Steps for the Future

No effective antidote has yet appeared for the ever-increasing problem of social withdrawal. This is a situation that almost never "cures itself"; meanwhile, even clinical cures are insufficient. Given this state of affairs, it seems clear that the number of people in withdrawal will only continue to increase from here on out. I hope that my thoughts about the hikikomori system help counteract this problem on the individual level, and well as on the level of the family, but at the same time, they should serve as a call for a more general, holistic response.

In 1991 the Japanese Ministry of Health and Welfare (Kōseishō) started a program called the "Model Project for Countermeasures for the Welfare of Withdrawn and Truant Children" *(Hikokomori-futōkō jidō fukushi taisaku moderu jigyō)*. It is shocking, however, that people eighteen or older are excluded from this project. This alone excludes over 90 percent of the cases of social withdrawal that I have described in this book, meaning that there is no way this project will be effective as a realistic countermeasure. In addition, we have a problem in the refusal of child counselors and educational counselors to see patients who are older than eighteen. And I have already repeated many times how poor the situation is for counseling centers—the main facilities that would ordinarily serve as the main resource for people in need.

In wrapping up this book, I would like to look at the big picture for a moment and make some suggestions in response to the current situation.

The first thing we must do is to make a concerted effort to raise awareness throughout society about social withdrawal and the situation surrounding it. Even though they often have no connections whatsoever between themselves, hikikomori patients are already emerging in large enough numbers that we can call social withdrawal a social phenomenon. I believe that in order to make that fact widely known, it is necessary for us to establish a solid definition of "social withdrawal" as a concept. Putting a firmly established diagnosis in place will likely make it easier to come up with countermeasures.

We must also extend our efforts to raise awareness about the issue within the world of psychiatry as well. The problem of social withdrawal is clearly one that psychiatric medicine should be dealing with. It is probably only a matter of time before this problem that we should be dealing with becomes one that we have no choice but to deal with. There is a problem, however. The Japanese Society of Psychiatry and Neurology (Nihon Seishin Shinkei Gakkai), the organization that extends the greatest influence over psychiatry in our country, has been extremely passive in regard to the problem of social withdrawal. I have presented at the Society twice about the hikikomori issue but, the first time, I received the response, "a withdrawal problem does not exist." The second time I presented, I was practically given the silent treatment. Perhaps I was not persuasive enough, but as the results of my survey showed, this issue does not seem to have been recognized yet as a psychiatric problem. To borrow the language of psychiatry itself, it seems that most psychiatrists have a tendency to engage in "denial," and isn't that in and of itself a kind of "withdrawal problem"?

I still have not given up, however. I will continue my own efforts to raise awareness about the issue in various ways, including writing books and articles. I am also thinking of using the Internet to strengthen my contacts with other psychiatrists and to work on developing a network to share information and collect knowledge. In any case, the most pressing work for us therapists is to join hands in helping others recognize this problem and accurately understand it. If we succeed in forming a network, then there will be hope even for people and families who live in areas where there are few counseling facilities available.

One possibility is that facilities that provide family counseling or family guidance, such as public health departments or other similar sites, could play a role in providing counseling. As I have suggested in this book, the first contact with the family of a patient going into withdrawal does not necessarily require an extremely high level of specialization or adaptivity. I cannot help but wonder how many people would be spared if, at the very beginning, families were just given even basic, commonsense help that they could take home and put into practice.

Another important issue is the creation of associations for families with children in withdrawal and "hangouts" for the hikikomori patients themselves. Right now, among the various activities I am engaging in to raise awareness and counsel people who need help, I am running a group for the families of hikikomori. If we are going to see the "withdrawal of the family" as part of the problem, as I have suggested we should, then it is necessary to bring together families who share the same problems; however, it is unfortunately the case that there are not yet really any facilities to help with social withdrawal specifically, even though recent years have seen a great increase in sites for people with psychological illnesses or problems attending school.

Still, we should not give up hope. Although the number is not yet large, associations are forming for families with hikikomori children. Until we have more associations available, it is probably possible for families to join family organizations designed for other psychological illnesses. There are organizations for families dealing with schizophrenia and substance abuse, and although those were designed for a different population, families might find it helpful to join those organizations, provided that they make it clear from the outset what the situation is.

Of course, it is imperative to provide and improve the quality of the facilities that will be receiving the hikikomori patients themselves. I expect that "hangouts" like the club I described before will increase in number, appearing in different localities all over the country. In addition, I have arranged for patients to get part-time jobs cleaning the local youth health center. Patients have said positive things about the experience, and in fact, this part-time job has served as the first step for quite a few of my patients on their path to successful employment. It is not especially difficult to place a person in a part-time job like that—one needs simply to give a simple explanation to the employer and to make sure that the employer pays more attention to absences and late arrivals than with other employees. More new possibilities will emerge for hikikomori patients if a greater number of understanding employers provide this kind of work environment.

There will likely be certain people who will still find themselves stuck, unable to leave the house, no matter how hard they and their families try. Work environments using computers should probably be prepared for such people. The number of people who work from home on the Internet is already on the rise. In an earlier chapter, I wrote that it is extremely significant to maintain connections with other people, even if it is only through the medium of computer communication. Similarly, the experience of getting a job and receiving compensation, if even only through the computer, will certainly lead to future developments.

One thing that we all can do, starting now, is to accept the reality of social withdrawal—a phenomenon that is growing right before our very eyes. This means attempting to recognize and understand the issue correctly, *not* trying to "deny" its existence through hasty criticism. I believe that the spread of this kind of understanding can help disengage hikikomori systems in deadlock and prevent the spread of new cases of withdrawal.

TRANSLATOR'S NOTES

Introduction

1. Saitō Tamaki, *"Hikikomori" kyūshutsu manyuaru* (Tokyo: PHP Kenkyūjo, 2001), 28–29. All Japanese names that appear in this book are in the traditional Japanese order, with surname first, then given name. For instance, Saitō is the surname, and Tamaki is the given name.

2. Ibid., 28–29.

3. Ibid., 29.

4. Ibid., 29–30.

5. Saitō Tamaki, *Hikikomori bunka ron* (Tokyo: Kinokuniya Shoten, 2003).

6. Richard Lloyd Parry, "This Man Won't Leave His Room, and He's Not Alone: Japan's Missing Million," *Independent,* December 5, 2000, 7.

7. See Doi Takeo, *The Anatomy of Dependence,* trans. John Bester (Tokyo: Kodansha, 1973).

8. Saitō, *"Hikikomori" kyūshutsu manyuaru,* 52–53; my translation.

Preface

1. BBC News, November 14, 2006, http://news.bbc.co.uk/2/hi/uk_news/6134920.stm.

2. Available online at http://www.ncgmkohnodai.go.jp/pdf/jidouseishin/22ncgm_hikikomori.pdf.

2. The Symptoms and Development of Social Withdrawal

1. "Not attending school" *(futōkō)* came into the spotlight as a major social issue in the late 1980s and 1990s, in conjunction with a number of other social issues affecting children and young adults: the high frequency of bullying in schools, high suicide rates, crimes committed by students who did not feel they fit into the system or had been skipping school, and concerns about the general quality of adolescent life.

2. As Saitō suggests, significant segments of the population pointed out that Japanese middle and high schools do not always provide a good environment for all students and that skipping school was a natural reaction to these environments. In this way, "nonattendance at school" developed into a political issue during the 1990s in particular.

3. In Japan the phobia of interpersonal relations *(taijin kyōfushō)* is frequently subdivided into four subcategories: the phobia of blushing *(sekimen kyōfu)*, the phobia of a deformed appearance *(shūbō kyōfu)*, the phobia of one's own body odor *(jiko shū kyōfu)*, and the phobia of one's own glance *(jiko shisen kyōfu)*. Each of these correlates to an existing concept in American psychiatry, except for the final fear of one's own glance, which does not match any preexisting category in the *DSM-IV* and thus has no English equivalent. See Yasuhide Iwata et al., "Jiko-shisen-kyofu (Fear of One's Own Glance), but Not Taijin-kyofusho (Fear of Interpersonal Relations), Is an East Asian Culture-Related Specific Syndrome," *Australian and New Zealand Journal of Psychiatry* 45, no. 2 (2011): 148–52.

4. Typically, contemporary Japanese public schools have six years of elementary school, three years of middle school, and three years of high school.

9. In Daily Life

1. Japanese has many pronouns that mean "you." These two pronouns are among them, but they are both diminutive and do not show respect for the addressee. The effect is much the same sort of direct bluntness seen in the expression "Hey you!" shouted out to someone in English.

2. In Japanese, people will often use the name of the addressee instead of pronouns, sometimes with the polite suffix *-san*, which shows a level of respect for the addressee. For instance, a speaker might say directly

to Mr. Tanaka, "Tanaka-*san*'s suit is very nice today." *Anata* is a pronoun meaning "you" that does not have the same bluntness and directness as the pronouns *kimi* and *omae*, which are both direct and diminutive.

3. The term that Saitō uses for what is translated "emotional dependence" is *amae*, which refers to the specific kind of affectionate dependence one feels when in a subordinate position. One might feel *amae* to a parent, a teacher, a lover who is more powerful or dominant. One aspect of *amae* is the desire to be loved in return in an almost unconditional way. The psychologist Doi Takeo has discussed this concept and its important position within Japanese society in great detail in the book *Amae no kōzō* (The anatomy of dependence).

11. Treatment and Returning to Society

1. This organization, which was a rough equivalent of the American National Alliance on Mental Illness, went bankrupt and dissolved in 2007.

12. The Social Pathology of Withdrawal

1. "The principle of three no's" was a term used in the 1970s to refer to the temperament of the Japanese youth: no drive, no interest, and no sense of responsibility.

2. *Otaku* is a Japanese word that describes people with passionate interests in subcultural things. The word *otaku* emerged in the 1970s, but it was during the 1980s that the life, well-being, and cultural contributions of *otaku* became an important social issue. Zenkyōtō was a student, self-governing group established during the height of the radical student protests of the 1960s. Zenkyōtō led strikes and even armed resistance at many major Japanese universities, disrupting the operations of schools and, in certain cases, even succeeding in taking over schools altogether for a period of time.

3. Japan's Ministry of Education, Culture, Sports, Science, and Technology (Monbukagakushō) states in their Basic Survey of Schools (Gakkō kihon chōsa), that in 1998, the year that Saitō first published this book, 36.4 percent of Japanese students continued from high school to four-year colleges, and 11.8 percent continued on from high school to two-year colleges. By 2009 the percentage of Japanese high school students continuing

to four-year colleges had risen to 50.2 percent, while the percentage of students continuing to two-year colleges had dropped to 6.0 percent. See http://www.mext.go.jp/b_menu/toukei/chousa01/kihon/1267995.htm. The rise of the number of students going to four-year colleges and the decrease of students going to two-year colleges has much to do with Japan's low birthrate. The number of students competing for spots at the four-year colleges has significantly decreased in recent years, meaning that more students are able to apply successfully to schools that might have been more difficult in the past. Meanwhile, smaller two-year colleges in Japan have been folding or reorganizing because of lack of enrollment.

4. The Japan Teachers Union (Nihon Kyōshokuin Kumiai, often shortened to Nikkyōso), Japan's largest labor union for teachers, has often leveled criticism at the conservative trends that have surfaced in postwar Japanese democracy. For instance, they have engaged in protests against history textbooks that talk little about Japanese involvement in World War II and against school policies that require the singing of the national anthem or standing to the national flag, both of which still retain strong wartime memories for many people.

BIBLIOGRAPHY

A short bibliography was included in the original Japanese edition of this book in 1998. Since then, many more studies about withdrawal and "hikikomori problems" have been published in Japan. At Saitō Tamaki's request, a selection of those books have been added here, along with texts mentioned in the translator's introduction.

Genda Yūji and Maganuma Mie. *Nīto, furītā demo shitugyōsha demo naku* (Neither NEET, freeter, nor unemployed). Tokyo: Gentōsha, 2004.

Hirose Tetsuya. "Tōhi-gata yokuutsu' ni tsuite" (On 'escapist-style' depression). In *Sōutsubyō no seishin byōri,* ed. Tadao Miyamoto, 61–86. Tokyo: Kōbundō, 1977.

Ide Sōhei. *Hikikomori no shakaigaku* (A sociology of withdrawal). Tokyo: Sekai Shisōsha, 2007.

Inamura Hiroshi. *Shishunki zasetsu shōkō gun* (Adolescent setback syndrome). Tokyo: Shin'yōsha, 1983.

———. *Tōkō kyohi no kokufuku* (Overcoming the refusal to go to school). Tokyo: Shin'yōsha, 1988.

———. *Wakamono apashī no jidai* (The era of youth apathy). Tokyo: Nihon Hōsō Kyōkai, 1989.

———. *Futōkō, hikikomori Q&A* (Not going to school/withdrawal Q&A). Tokyo: Seishin Shobō, 1993.

Ishii Kan'ichirō and Kasahara Yomishi, eds. *Suchūdento apashī* (Student apathy). Special issue of *Gendai no esupuri* (Contemporary spirit) 168 (1981).

Kano Rikihachirō and Kondō Naoji, eds. *Seinen no hikikomori: Shinri shakaiteki haikei, byōri, chiryō enjo* (Adolescents in withdrawal: Psychological and social background, pathology, and support for treatment). Tokyo: Iwasaki Gakujutsu Shuppansha, 2000.

Kasahara Yomishi. *Apashī shindorōmu: Kōgakureki shakai no seinen shinri* (Apathy syndrome: The psychology of young adults in a society of high educational achievement). Tokyo: Iwanami Shoten, 1984.

———. *Taikyaku shinkeishō: Mukiryoku, mukanshin, mukairaku no kokufuku* (Retreat neurosis: Overcoming apathy, disinterest, and the lack of pleasure). Kōdansha Gendai Shinshō 901. Tokyo: Kōdansha, 1988.

Machizawa Shizuo. *Tobenai tonbo no shinri ryōhō* (How to heal the psychology of the dragonfly that cannot fly). Tokyo: PHP Kenkyūjo, 1996.

Nakai Hisao and Yasuhiro Yamanaka, eds. *Shishunki no seishin byōri to chiryō* (The pathology and treatment of adolescent psychology). Tokyo: Iwasaki Gakujutsu Shuppansha, 1978.

Narita Yoshihiro. *Kyōhakusei-shō no rinshō kenkyū* (Clinical research on obsessive-compulsive disorder). Tokyo: Kongō Shuppan, 1994.

Saitō Tamaki. *"Hikikomori" kyūshutsu manyuaru* (How to rescue your child from "hikikomori"). Tokyo: PHP Kenkyūjo, 2002.

———. *Hikikomori bunka ron* (On the culture of withdrawal). Tokyo: Kinokuniya Shoten, 2003.

———. *Shakaiteki hikikomori: Owaranai shishunki* (Social withdrawal: Adolescence without end). Tokyo: PHP Shinsho, 1998.

Tanaka Chieko. *Hikikomori: "Taiwa suru kankei" o torimodosu tame ni* (Withdrawal: What to do to restore a "conversational relationship"). Tokyo: Saiensusha, 1996.

Tomita Fujiya. *Hikikomori kara no tabidachi* (Setting forth on a journey from withdrawal). Tokyo: Hāto Shuppan, 1992.

———. *Chichi no hitokoto ga boku o kaeta* (A single word from my father changed me). Tokyo: Hāto Shuppan, 1993.

———. *Hikikomori to tōkō, shūshoku kyohi, ijime Q&A* (Q&A on withdrawal, the refusal to go to school or work, and bullying). Tokyo: Hāto Shuppan, 1996.

Walters, Paul A. "Student Apathy." In *Emotional Problems of the Student*, ed. Graham B. Blaine and Charles C. McArthur, 129–47. New York: Appleton-Century-Crofts, 1971.

Zenkoku Seishin Shōgaisha Kazoku Kai Rengōkai, ed. *Zenkoku shakai shigen meibo '95–'97* (Register of names of social resources throughout the country). Tokyo: Seishin Shōgaisha Shakai Fukki Sokushin Sentā, 1995.

Zielenziger, Michael. *Shutting Out the Sun: How Japan Created Its Own Lost Generation*. New York: Nan A. Talese, 2006.

———. *Hikikomori no kuni: Naze Nihon wa "ushinawareta" seiyo o unda no ka* (Land of hikikomori: Why Japan gave birth to a "lost" generation). Trans. Kōno Junji. Tokyo: Kōbunsha, 2007.

INDEX

SAITŌ TAMAKI is a practicing psychiatrist and director of medical services at Sōfūkai Sasaki Hospital in Funabashi, Japan. He is the author of more than two dozen books, including *Beautiful Fighting Girl*, published in English by the University of Minnesota Press in 2011.

JEFFREY ANGLES is associate professor of modern Japanese literature and translation at Western Michigan University. He is author of *Writing the Love of Boys: Origins of Bishōnen Culture in Modernist Japanese Literature* (Minnesota, 2011) and translator of *Twelve Views from the Distance* by Mutsuo Takahashi (Minnesota, 2012).